TORREN

WELCOME to anoth e
become a regular f
angling writers an n
and in great form.

There's a witty insight into the world of matchman FRANK BARLOW and an eye-witness account from MIKE MILLMAN on the rigours of wrecking way over the horizon.

DAVE COSTER gives a no-nonsense summary of complex baiting trends while prolific angling author TREVOR HOUSBY reports from an island paradise just 40 minutes flying time from Southampton where divers have come face to face with wrasse that would make anybody gasp.

You'll discover why Avington trout lakes exert such a strong grip on the angling life of former world champion TONY PAWSON and which shore fishing spots are rated as superior by BOB GLEDHILL who has fished the lot.

Get the message? As always, virtually every sphere of angling is reflected in your favourite Annual. . . and among the entertainment there's masses of fundamental advice including detailed descriptions for making-up terminal rigs recommended by the Mail's team of stars.

One final word of encouragement before you start browsing through our 1988 line-up. The face of angling has been fast changing in recent seasons with a torrent of technical advances in tackle confusing a good many as to the correct way to progress in the sport.

But in reality it isn't absolutely necessary to know every modern dodge to succeed with rod and line. FRED CROUCH has been using the same barbel methods for 30 years and he catches just as many big 'uns in this hi-tech age as he ever did. In this Annual he looks back over his lifetime's pursuit of a single species.

At heart, fishing is a marvellous individual sport. The extent of the challenge can largely be of your own making. Long may it continue to offer such freedom of choice.

ROY WESTWOOD
EDITOR

MY TOP TEN SHORE SPOTS

BOB GLEDHILL has fished
coastline. These are the spo

FILEY BRIGG

THE Brigg is a half-mile long rocky outcrop in Yorkshire between Bridlington and Scarborough. Its appeal is versatility. There are fish around it for most of the year.

Cod are always in casting distance but summer visitors include wrasse, mackerel and dogfish. In winter there's also whiting, dabs and coalfish.

The ground is fairly tough on tackle so use fairly heavy line such as 25lb. Best fishing is on the south side, and the further along you walk, the better your chances.

Fish it on the outgoing tide and at low water, and back up the Brigg when the tide starts to flood over.

Crab baits are best for the cod and coalfish, but worm will take most species. Lugworm can be dug at low water alongside the Brigg.

Filey Brigg is tough on tackle

WESTON-SUPER-MARE

THE Old Pier in Weston is a highly-rated and very consistent mark. Spring to early winter is the best time.

Summer species are conger eel, rays, mackerel, big packs of dogfish and flatties. In the autumn and early winter whiting and then cod come within casting range.

Best baits are those with a high fish content. Plain mackerel strip works best for the congers, but try squid and lugworm cocktails for the dogs and rays.

The pier enjoys a rightful reputation as a mark where the fish are high on quality. Double-figure rays are not uncommon and while the congers are mainly 5lb to 15lb, there are plenty of them.

STAR TIP *Try to fish over low water which produces much more fish.*

SOUTHEND PIER

IF I had to nominate the most obliging mark in Essex it would have to be this mile-long pier.

It provides encouragement for the newcomer with flounders and mackerel. For the more experienced there are big bass at night. There is also a real prospect of golden grey mullet.

The mullet like bunches of small ragworm while the top bass bait is a big, jelly-soft peeler crab. Try floatfishing with the lightest tackle you have for garfish and mackerel.

In winter there are the whiting and dabs, with the flatties loving juicy lugworm. There are also cod and lug is the bait to use for these.

There is no tackle shop on the pier now — the last one was chopped in half by a boat that smashed into the pier! But there are several tackle shops within a few hundred yards of the pier entrance and they all sell bait.

STAR TIP *If you want to try for a winter cod, go for the East Point.*

cores of shore marks over the years right around Britain's hat impressed him the most.

FALMOUTH

FALMOUTH harbour offers the opportunity to fish from rock marks, piers, harbour walls, beaches and estuaries.

In the centre of the town is the Prince of Wales Pier and Custom House Quay. Fish with worm or peeler crab for flounders, small bass and pollack. Spinning will produce mackerel for much of the year and a better class of pollack.

If it's wrasse you are after then few places match Pendennis Point. Crab is way out in front as bait and you can either float fish or leger.

Fish around here at night with mackerel strip and there is every chance of a conger. Spinning from the Pendennis area produces lively mackerel and in summer, garfish.

For some fun flounder fishing try the River Fal estuary, using crab or worm bait. There's even the chance of a plaice or two here.

Mullet by the million all around the bay — but just try and catch 'em!

STAR TIP *When collecting crabs for wrasse fishing save hard ones — wrasse take them eagerly.*

RIVER TYNE

THE River Tyne estuary is one of the most popular marks in the North East of England where canny Geordies catch fish all the year round.

Most popular mark on the north bank is the Bergen ferry landing jetty. This is in constant use during the week and there is no fishing.

Come Sunday, there is no sailing and it gets over-run with anglers! The fishing is dominated by coalfish, which are caught throughout the year.

From September through to May, codling also show up and it is not unknown for anglers to get over a dozen cod a session.

On the south bank the main mark is the small breakwater at South Shields called the Groyne. Here, there is good sport with coalfish, and codling often show up among them.

Best bait is peeler crab, but worm will always take fish.

STAR TIP *The best of the cod fishing is always early in the morning before the boat traffic gets busy.*

PEEL, ISLE OF MAN

ANYBODY who takes their holiday on this island in the Irish Sea has the chance to fish a very versatile mark.

The best fishing is off the end of Peel Breakwater, where there are some super coalfish. The method is freelining a piece of mackerel.

Light spinning gear will cope as no casting is involved — the bait is just lobbed out. The coalfish dart at the bait as it sinks slowly and naturally through the water.

A stroll around the back of Peel Castle leads to a rocky shoreline that is good for wrasse with worm and crab baits. Spinning produces pollack and mackerel here.

STAR TIP *If ever you see the kipper factory dumping herring offal over the side of the breakwater, the water will explode with feeding coalfish!*

Brian Fawcett, of Liverpool, shows the stamp of thornback that can be caught from the shore in North Wales on the Lleyn Peninsula

LLEYN PENINSULA

TWELVE miles of sand and rock lying south of Caernarvan in Snowdonia, North Wales. Excellent area for quality as well as variety.

Northern end of the Peninsula is mainly sand and fishes best in the evening and at night, over high water. Expect to take thornback rays, bass, plenty of whiting and dogs and occasional tope.

Worms and fish strip are the best bait.

The bottom end of the Lleyn is quite rocky and produces good pollack fishing on floatfished worm and spinners. There is good wrasse fishing near Bardsy Sound.

A pleasant place to spend an evening's fishing is Trefor Pier, where you can offer mackerel strip for dogs, small conger eels and even a bull huss or two.

Very much an all-year round fishery, but best from spring to Christmas.

STAR TIP *Helpful information from Nefyn tackle shop. Telephone 0758 720815.*

MY TOP TEN continued

ARNSIDE

ONE of the most prolific flounder marks to be found anywhere in Britain. Arnside overlooks the estuary of the River Kent amid the beautiful hills of the Lake District in Cumbria.

Sport peaks when the tide is out and the fish are concentrated in the river that is left. Fishing season is from summer through to January but September to Christmas is the most hectic when bags of 30lb are not uncommon.

Best baits are worms and small fish strips occasionally do well. Favourite tackle is a simple two-hook leger rig with just enough weight to hold bottom.

The tide flow is very strong at times, so take wired sinkers. Do not cast a long way. The best of the flounder fishing is just 20 yards out. The further out you cast the shallower the water gets.

Most productive area is around the old boatyard, downstream of the railway bridge. Another hot-spot is the by the stream that flows out of a garden wall and across the bank.

Arnside the tiny Cumbria estuary that is paved with flounders.

HURST CASTLE

THIS is a 1½-mile finger of shingle that juts out into the Western Solent in Hampshire. Its appeal is the variety of fish it offers.

Reach it by walking from Milford or catch a ferry from Keyhaven.

In summer big shoals of mackerel and garfish mass in Hurst Hole and they can be taken either spinning or floatfishing. For the patient there are some cracking bass, with fresh sandeel by far the best bait.

At night, the same area is highly rated for Dover sole. Use fish bait and there are sporting congers, plenty of dogs and a good chance of a ray or two.

BALCARY POINT, SOUTH-WEST SCOTLAND

A cod hooked from Balcary point in Scotland — the best shore mark in the UK.

UNQUESTIONABLY the greatest shore mark in Britain for big cod. Reach it driving through Dumfries and then head for the coast. Best chance of a monster cod is from November to March. Daylight produces as many fish as darkness and it is much safer and more comfortable.

There's no need to cast a long way, and terminal tackle can be a simple two-hook trace with 3/0 hooks and Breakaway sinker.

Pick of the fishing is from the rock platforms that are exposed at low water, but there are also several good perches for fishing at high water.

Best bait is lugworm, with as many on the hook as you can cram!

There are no cod in summer, but still worth a day out for the plaice, dogs and rays that swim by. Use worm and fish baits for these.

STAR TIP

Always take a long-handled gaff — some monster fish have been lost for the want of one!

These trout are out of bounds

Peter Cockwill and rainbows hooked near the floating cages at Bewl Water in Kent. He knows they're tiddlers compared to the giants lurking out of reach beneath those floating cages!

PETER COCKWILL on the big fish that lurk beneath rearing cages

THE rearing on of trout in suspended net cages is now a familiar sight on our major trout reservoirs and also many small water fisheries.

There are benefits and not a few drawbacks to this system, but let's first look at the positive advantages to both angler and manager.

The most obvious factor is that fish reared on site will already be acclimatised to the water and stocking is therefore relatively simple. It's just a matter of tipping them into the lake or, with a large water, giving them a ride in a boat before release.

Buying in small fish is relatively cheap compared to stockable ones and they can be delivered in a single consignment. This immediately reduces transport costs compared to a more conventianal once or twice weekly input of takeable sized fish.

Growing on the fish with regular feeds of pellet is a relatively inexpensive way of producing stockies compared to buying them in although careful consideration should be given to the labour element involved.

While I realise that water authorities are nowadays more cost conscious, I question the availability of using high powered boats to roar out across the lake at regular intervals for the feeding process and also the apparent need to double man this operation.

Fish constantly available on site also means that trickle stocking can be simply achieved to maintain a constant level of fishing.

On the debit side of this cage system of rearing fish is the ecological impact of the instant output of waste products from the fish.

The area immediately under cages is most always completely barren while elsewhere the lake may suffer prolific weed growth due to excess nitrogenous waste build up or may suffer an almost constant algae bloom in the warmer months.

It is well recognised that cages are a holding area for large fish which rarely venture far from their cover. This was clearly proven when some very large individual browns and rainbows were taken from close to the Rutland cages.

However, aways conscious that the punter mustn't do too well, resevoirs now prohibit boats from a 100 yard ring around the cages on the basis that hooks in the nets are a danger to the operators.

Undoubtedly this is a real danger, but 100 yards does mean that a lot of fish just never get cropped. It seems such a waste to let magnificent specimens live out their lives with little prospect of them being caught.

While I also realise that the 100 yard regulations must be enforced, it becomes more than a little tedious on some waters to be constantly haranged by bailiffs even when wind variations cause an anchored boat to swing inside the arbituary line.

It seems to me that if reservoirs really are intent on keeping anglers away from the cages then they should either moor them inside the nature reserve bays or very close to the boat jetties and have set up at least a 200 yard exclusion zone.

This latter situation would also reduce the need to constantly exercise speedboats and might even provide a bit more time for some effective anti poaching/cheating activities.

A snatch take puts a good bend in Peter's rod. He'd anchored up 100 yards away from the Bewl cages hotspot and that's as close as anybody can get.

TOP GEAR

HOW CARPMAN KEVIN NASH SETS ABOUT CATCHING SPECIMENS TO 40lb.

THE pace of change in fishing tackle design can leave you well behind the times if you sit staring at your float too long! This is particularly true in carp fishing where the ingenuity of specimen hunters has helped put bigger fish on the bank over recent seasons.

KEVIN NASH is among the country's leading carp anglers with a career best fish of more than 40lb to his credit. He described his tackle as part of the Top Gear series published in the Mail...

My favourite hook is the eyed Mustad O'Shaughnessy. It is heavy in the wire and forged making it very strong. The eye is neat and the barb not too large. I have confidence in it — an important point when I have to lean hard into a heavy fish. I find the sizes 6, 8 and 10 most useful.

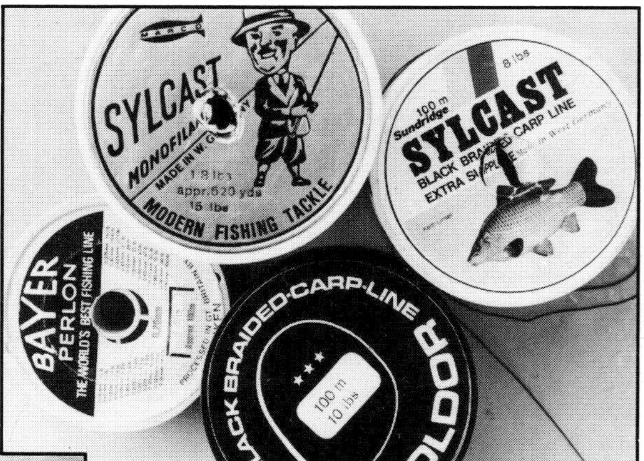

Main line of about 9lb will cover most eventualities. In weedy or snaggy waters a heavier line of 15lb line is advisable. When casting heavy leads a long way it is essential to use a 30ft shock leader of 15lb to prevent crackoffs. This is tied to the main line using a four-turn Water Knot or Double-tucked Blood Knot.

I generally use braided hook lengths of 8lb or 10lb. Braided line is much more supple than nylon. For tying my hair-rigs I use nylon of between 4lb and 5lb.

I carry a selection of leads between 1¾ oz and 2½ oz. These may seem rather heavy to most anglers, but besides long-range casting, the weights play an important role in the end rigs and their hooking efficiency.

It's important to be comfortable on long sessions. I use a Kevin Maddocks adjustable bedchair to sit and sleep on. I set it up so that I can reach and strike all my rods the moment a run develops.

Rods of between 1½ lb and 2½ lb test curve are ideal for carp fishing. A general rule for optimum casting weights is the *pound* to *ounce* rule. For example, a 1¾ lb test rod will handle leads to 1¾ oz. Overload a rod and you risk breaking it. Reels should have a large spool capable of holding over 100 yards of 10lb line.

My rods are supplied by Alan Brown. They are 12 foot carbons with a test curve of 2¼ lb. They'll cast well over 100 yards but have an easy through-action suitable for fishing closer ranges.

I prefer an audible alarm. It allows me to keep an eye on the water, and take a quick nap on long sessions. These buzzers are made by Andy Little and bleep when the line moves and causes the rollers to turn.

▲ When using more than one rod it is important that they are well organized. I set mine up on stainless steel buzzer bars. The rods should be set level or pointing down slightly in the general direction of the baits.

This is the Shimano Bait Runner reel with a switch at the back that sets the spool to revolve freely at a pre-determined amount of pull. This allows me to fish with the bail arm closed and the anti-reverse on. When the fish runs with bait it is fed line until I flick the switch and strike.

I use a monkey climber with my buzzers. This is set up in front of the reel, and consists of a steel rod and a drilled PTFE bobbin. The bobbin is fairly heavy keeping the line taut between buzzer and reel. If a fish should pick up a bait and run towards you the bobbin will drop back causing the buzzer to sound,

Remember that with other types of reel you must fish with an open bail arm so fish can take line freely. Strike as soon as you can.

TOP GEAR

Like most carp anglers I use the hair-rig. The chief advantage of the hair is that the hook hangs outside the bait where the carp is more likely to feel it and bolt.

To make a hair, I use 4lb line over which I slip a short piece of my own rig tube. The thin tubing is now passed over the hook point and up the shank, so trapping the hair against the hook. To one end of the hair is tied a neat loop with a knot at the other *(see Diag. A)*

This method allows me to adjust the hair length by pulling the hair at either end. About 1½ in. is right.

Note that the hair comes from the top or eye of the hook. This increases hooking efficiency when the bait is being blown out of the carp's mouth. *(Diag. B)*

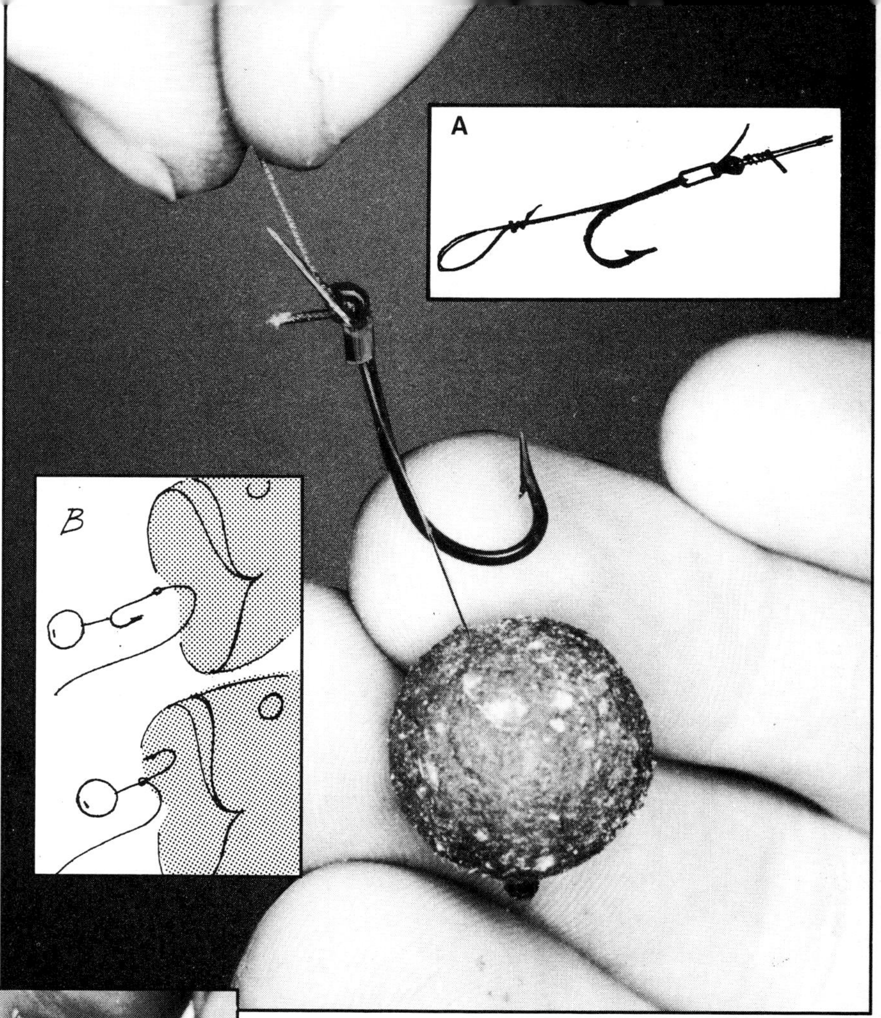

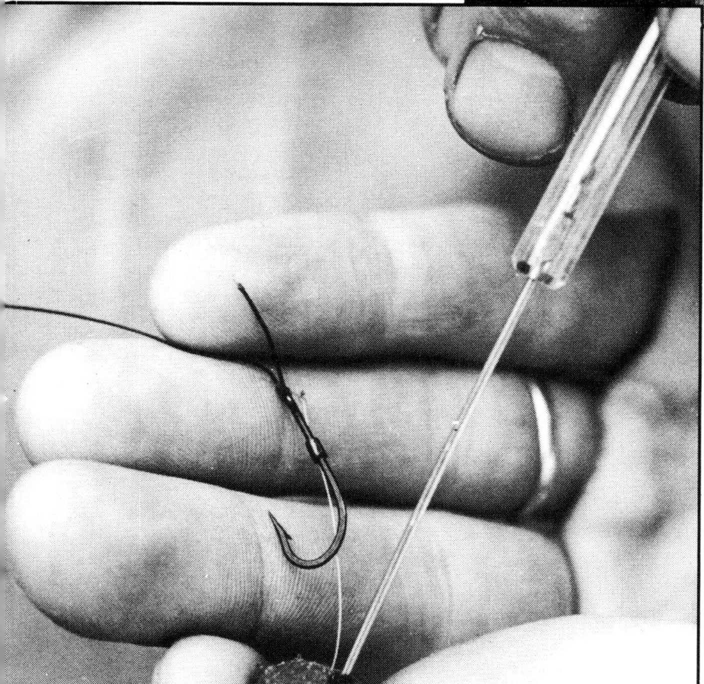

To push the loop of the hair through the bait I use a baiting needle. A piece of plastic or grass stalk is then passed through the loop and trapped against the boilie or particle preventing it from flying free.

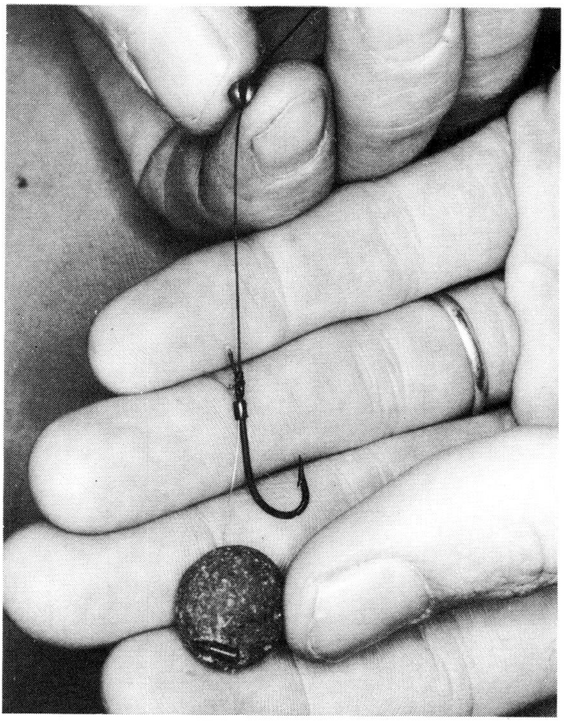

Boilies can be made to float by placing them in an oven or micro wave. Take a few out every couple of minutes and test them in a mug of water. They are very effective over a soft weedy bottom. Pinch a split shot onto the hooklength to anchor the bait just above the weed or mud.

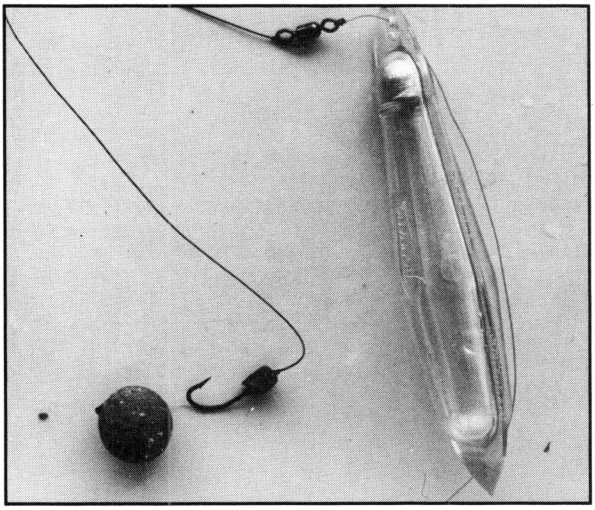

Surface baits tend to be light and difficult to cast and I use a controller. This one is an elongated bubble float. It is loaded at one end and casts like a rocket. Controllers can be made from pike floats quite easily. Remember to watch out for birds — seagulls and ducks are partial to floater as well as carp.

I use a hair-rig with my floaters and to stop the hook from sinking below the bait I hook on a small square of foam over the eye.

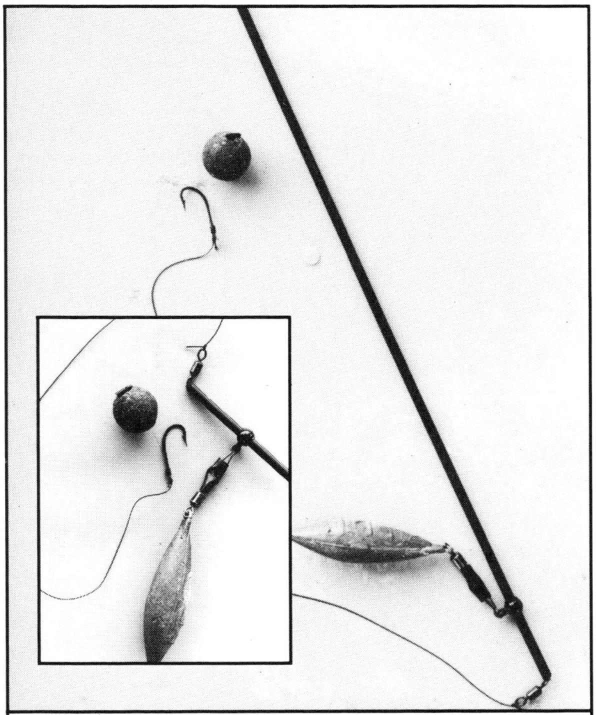

My normal rig consists of a Kevin Nash anti-tangle rig stopped by a swivel. The hook length is 8 or 10lb braided line. Braided line is far more supple than nylon and allows the bait to move more naturally when being sucked up by a carp.

The anti-tangle rig ensures that the easily tangled braided hook-length doesn't get wrapped about the main line.

It is important that the hook length is shorter than the tubing. About 9 to 12in. is about right. The bomb is attached to the leger link fixed on the tubing. Note the plastic sleeve I've placed over the link *(inset)*. This prevents it catching up in the landing net.

◀ One item I wouldn't be without is PVA string. This melts in water and I use it as a type of swimfeeder depositing boilies with pin point accuracy close to the hook bait. I tie a knot in one end, thread on three or four boilies and then tie the PVA to the hook. It is a useful ploy in the winter when carp don't search about so much for their food.

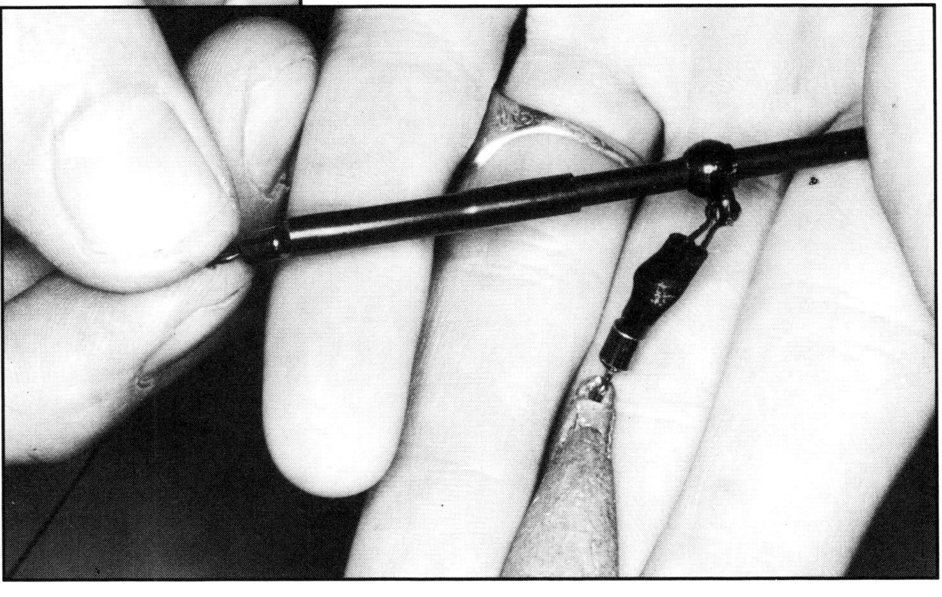

If I decide to fish a bolt-rig I slip a short length of tubing over the anti-tangle rig and swivel so stopping the line from running through. When a carp takes it jerks against the fixed lead causing it to bolt and hook itself in the process. Should the fish snap you it can rid itself of the lead with a sharp tug.

Liverpool's Dave Houghton nomina in his patch which are a cut above

CARR MILL

A crowded corner of Carr Mill Dam in summer.

FEARS that a keepnet ban on Carr Mill Dam would gradually drive anglers away have proved unfounded. Despite the ban on nets for pleasure fishing, anglers keep turning up and will carry on doing so while this Merseyside fishery continues to provide good fishing.

Take your choice and catch the fish. Patterns change through summer and winter but it is still a matter of selecting any one of several simple methods depending upon whether you are pleasure fishing, taking part in a team match, or going all-out for personal glory with a net of bream.

St. Helens AA who have bought the lake, make good use of the dog-legged shaped water for contests.

The main tactic in matches is to seek small roach and skimmer bream close in with three or four sections of a roach pole.

But Carr Mill Dam, situated alongside the main East Lancashire Road carrying heavy traffic between Liverpool and Manchester, is also a haven for pleasure anglers.

In summer local kids crowd the shallow shoreline on the west bank learning quickly how to catch shy biting bream which seldom run to more than 12oz.

Others mimic the matchmen and delight in spending five or six hours hooking 2oz roach cast after cast on 22's and a single or double squatt as bait.

It's a good way to master the basics yet if they went to the opposite end of the Dam they could be putting together a double-figure weight of decent bream.

The road end is popular because the car park is right alongside the bank. But the northern end is more pleasant from a scenic point of view.

Under normal conditions this is the most productive area in winter - especially close to the Arches Bridge. In summer it doesn't seem to matter where you fish.

Occasionally the anglers talk of catching 50 or 60lb of bream, and even the kids can finish with 5lb of small stuff. That's great fishing for such a heavily populated area.
Carr Mill Dam is for St Helens A.A. members only but annual cards are available from Jimmy Corkish, 65 Laffak Road, Carr Mill, St Helens.

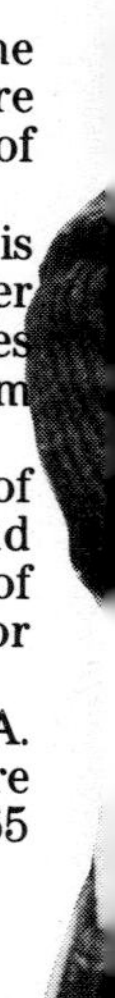

Pete Bramwell of St Helens AA with proof that the Carr Mill Dam bream come in all sizes!

s two waters average

DAM

A good place to master the basics

All methods will work on this Merseyside fishery including long range feeder tactics.

Searching for small roach on the pole in the Carr Mill shallows —you'd never think the main East Lancs Road was over the bank

Gresford Flash

Crucians have taken over

I USED to fish Llay AA's Gresford Flash near Wrexham as a schoolboy and I'll always remember my first session. It wasn't that I had such a good day, — there were only two small tench in my net at the end of the misty Sunday morning. But others had caught plenty.

Tench used to be the main fish and the best swims were between the lily beds on the roadside along one short side of the shallow lake. We always went early, but never early enough to get on the hot spots until someone tired of catching tench and moved away.

One day I managed to squeeze on the end of the road section alongside a line of reeds. After a while I noticed that the reeds were continuously moving despite there being no wind so I decided to have a forage with my landing net. Out came a dozen small crucian carp in a single sweep!

There must have millions of the brightly coloured carp because successive probes gave the same result. I left for home with my head full of plans for catching those crucians on rod and line.

It never happened. Gresford was a 40-mile journey from my home in Liverpool and on the few occasions when I did manage to persuade my father to go there, conditions were never the same.

Twenty years on and my personal circumstances have changed. A car gives the opportunity to fish many waters and I finally decided it was high time I had another go at Gresford.

The idea struck me when I was having an afternoon's grueller on the Shropshire Union Canal with Len Bolton. He wasn't over impressed with spending a break from his busy butcher's shop in Birkenhead to struggle for a few small fish.

'We should have gone to Gresford', he said, 'The place is fishing really well.'

He didn't have to repeat the suggestion, and the following Wednesday afternoon we were running the car into an almost deserted car park up the road from the Flash. Adding his expertise to the trip was Eddie Simpson from Ellesmere Port.

The roadside swims were empty but the lads advised that the best fishing came from the side bank. The only other major change is that the tench have been replaced by hordes of hard-fighting crucian carp.

We moved up the well worn path and settled down on comfortable bank between margin reed. There's no need to go much further than the end of the weed with the tackle so my choice of rig was for a small loaded float, a medium wire 18's and 1½lb line.

Eddie used the same rig while Len's bottom gear was similar but he used a pole and flick tip.

It was a slow start with only a small roach and gudgeon showing interest in the combinations of maggot and caster. Then a couple of nice crucian carp were captured and it was the signal Len wanted. He switched completely to caster.

He used two on the hook and loose fed every cast with about half-a-dozen and gradually worked up the swim until the fish were drawn into the water that was no more than 18 inches deep.

By this time the three of us were catching steadily but Eddie and I had to make do with the odd crucian in between a succession of gudgeon and roach.

Len was getting into a pattern. Now and again his float wouldn't settle as it dropped on to the back of the carp twisting and turning in front of him. It all became so easy.

If you fancy a day on the Flash then you'll have to join Llay AA. No day-tickets are issued. Applications for full membership are welcomed and should be sent to Derek Cornish, 200 Chester Road, Wrexham, Clwyd.

Eddie Simpson of Ellesmere Port with his Gresford net of crucians.

Len Bolton steers a carp to hand among the margin reed at Gresford Flash.

Frank Barlow's weekend report

Nottingham matchman FRANK BARLOW has drawn a huge following with his down-to-earth column in the Mail. Here's a taste of vintage Frank...

FIVE HOURS OF MISERY

Something to smile about for a change. Frank had this two-hour catch from the Trent at Nottingham... from the same swim he fished as a kid.

WELCOME once more to 'Gruellers Weekly'. Over the past few months with very few exceptions I have had some shocking luck, but this weekend really took the biscuit.

It started on Saturday, the first match in Rip Off's Saturday Long Higgin series.

The days when they used to call this bank 'Frank's Bank' seemed light years away as I once again drew a right cesspit.

The first match was of only 67 pegs, that is all the Parkside AC water. As most Higgin-men know, there are 66 pegs on the Parkside and one, No. 67 at the bottom of the Manvers water. Right first time — in I went and out came 67.

I have been fishing this length for as long as I care to remember, and this peg has only won any coin on two occasions and that's when there's a bad east wind, for then you are slightly sheltered.

Today the wind was downstream and into your face, which brought leaves the size of dinner plates going past in a never ending stream.

I started on the float, but at 14ft deep, two feet from the bank it was really a hopeless situation. Two roach in the first hour then the leaves were impossible, every cast resulted in a propeller on the end of your line.

It was so bad that team-mate 'Gizz-a-Fag' Don who was three pegs away packed in, he could not do a thing with it.

Every so often on my peg there are a few chub caught, so I decided to stick it out to the end on the feeder. A long rod held in the air to miss the leaves, and a small Drennan job with extra lead on, produced a lightning bite every cast from skimmers of around 2 oz, apiece.

At the end of probably the most miserable five hours I ever had on the Higgin, I had amassed 35 of these, three roach and eight gudgeon for 3lb plus — a total waste of time as the first 50 pegs had all had the wind favourable and were catching odd fish all day.

As so often happens on a hard day here, peg No 1 near the yacht club won the match with 11lb of chub, then there were a lot of weights between 5 lb and 7 lb.

Despite all my moaning I still think it's the most even length on the river — I was just in the wrong place at the wrong time.

The previous Wednesday I had won my section with 8lb odd of roach at peg 52 so Saturday's result was all the harder to take having gone geared up expecting to catch.

As I walked back across the meadow, I had to pass a travelling circus that performs yearly in the area. There was this huge camel with two humps grazing outside the big top. It looked just like Pete Clapperton without glasses and do you know, I'm sure it was grinning at me. It probably would have had more out of peg 67 than me the way I'm fishing.

SUN

Somebody moved flyer

COME Sunday and I'm on my way to Cropthorne on the Warwick Avon for the third round of the West Midlands Winter league.

Yesterday's disappointments cast aside I was looking forward to a few fish here, but if you think the Higgin was bad for me, you will not believe what today had in store.

I arrived in good time at the draw to witness the plastic egg brigade in action again. I'm sure the portions were even smaller this time, but I warned them didn't I?

Stan put his hand in and drew us No.11 in section. At least we had one good draw because No. 11 is always two pegs below the weir at Cropthorne and with this league being decided on weight you must have a couple of flyers to do any good. In fact this peg is rarely out of the first three in matches here.

I could not believe my luck when I opened my ticket to see No.11 gazing at me. Yesterday's grueller seemed 50 years ago as the lads who knew it gave me all the info I needed.

A quick check on the map confirmed it as two below the weir, so off I set for this flyer.

Now it's a long trek to the weir down a lane, over a railway, down a steep hill, then across the fields. I must have seemed like a fat Seb Coe and I reckon I broke all records for getting there.

When I eventually arrived it's a good job there were no law officers about. The Avon Valley was, I'm sorry to say, blue, I really cracked up.

Instead of two below the weir I was five pegs above it — 16ft deep and anglers opposite all throwing the plastic pig over the river.

I pulled myself together and decided to give it my best shot. This was not helped when the chap who drew the peg below me took one look and promptly cleared off, saying how useless it was.

The lads on the other bank were getting the odd fish so I cheered up a bit. I started on the waggler about halfway across this side of where the feeders were going in. This bought a ruffe and a gudgeon on the first two casts. At least I was weighing in.

After half-an-hour the float disappeared and I had a 'dog' on. It went over the river for 15 long minutes before finally breaking me in a snag under the rod end. I was racked off!

The straight lead and feeder were tried every so often, but the only bites I could get were on the float that is, when the rowers allowed me to cast in as they were using my peg to turn round in!

Halfway through I had a chub of 2½lb, then five small roach to finish with 2lb 11oz for fourth in the section. Two below the weir was second with 14 lb.

Wayne Swinscoe was our best weight with 9 lb in a disaster day for my Shakespeare team. We finished fifth with 39lb.

Cardiff won again as they had a 19 lb and 13 lb, which leaves us one point clear at the top with three to go, all at Eckington. I can't wait!

There's plenty of beef behind that rod to deal with anything that swims!

WARMER IN SIBERIA

SAT

I WELL remember the days when the first two weeks of September were the most reliable for good weather. We always used to save our holidays for those weeks and they always used to coincide with the Trent fish feeding well.

Not so this weekend. Saturday I took the long journey to Bridgwater, Somerset, to fish the National Federation of Anglers' South West Region Championship on the Huntspill. I cannot imagine Siberia being much warmer. I was perished.

My Shakespeare team were representing our club, Glevum AC, and we dearly wanted a trophy because we thought it would look nice on Mr Tomsett's desk — he's the boss man of our sponsors.

I drew the end peg in A section of the pump house next to Woolavington Bridge and a nice surprise was waiting at my peg in the shape of a huge diesel water pump.

The peg was a good yard away from its exhaust pipe which was belching out blue, rancid fumes. It was deafening and the thought of five hours next to this really teed me off. Then, mysteriously, it stopped. Enough said about that!

By now, the river had got up and rollers were blowing down the river. The colour looked horrible and all the signs pointed to a grueller. For 90 per cent of the field that is what it turned out to be.

I started on the waggler and after sorting the depth out, which turned out to be 2½ft in the middle, I started getting the odd roach and after an hour I had nine.

Then the wind got worse, pushing the float upstream against the flow. Lead, feeder all were tried but all I could do in the remaining four hours was to muster an eel and a Tommy to finish with just 1 lb 10 oz. This put me second in the section of 16. Welsh International Ken Hornsey won the section with 2 lb 1oz.

I must do something about him as that's three times he's pipped me in the last couple of years. Once he beat me on the Gloucester Canal with a flounder of all things and at the time I would have sworn it came from Tiger Bay.

A fine angler is Ken, thank God he lives in Cardiff. The rest of the lads did well in their sections and we totalled 140 points to win the match by five points.

We were dead chuffed when it worked out right. It makes the 360 mile round trip worth it and just about covers your expenses. A word of praise for the NFA officials, a very well organised and smoothly run job.

SUN

Home to roost

Frank's tackle box... on one of its better days!

AFTER Saturday's long haul a home match was definitely on the cards. A ten minute drive to Rip Off's weekly Open at Attenboro'.

The draw held a nice surprise in the shape of Steve's wife 'Mrs Rip Off' alias Angie. Instead of the usual slagging-off from him it's nice to be treated with civility and courtesy.

Why doesn't Steve clear off to other matches more often?

I pulled out No. 6. Now that has got bream form — two caught in the last five matches — but seven and eight have won more coin than any other and are currently the fliers. At least I was in the area.

My plan was to fish for bream on the feeder whilst feeding loose maggots on the float line. The first hour produced three perch and a roach on the feeder but on peg seven in-form Trevor Blair had taken three bream and Stu Killen on eight had two. On peg five to my right Shoes had two.

Well, I felt a proper Wilf. So I put on a heavier feeder and cast as far as I could in the facing wind. That would be about 40 yards.

This was followed by six balls of feed, not the done thing on the pits this season, but being behind I thought S or B.

Within 15 minutes I had a bream of about 3 lb followed quickly by one a bit bigger. That wiped the smile off Shoes' boatrace.

A quick look on the waggler did not produce a bite, probably because it was 13ft at the rod end, not right for roach.

With one and a half hours to go I had another fish which shed the hook just as I was about to net it. It just laid there on the surface so I duly scooped it out. About time I had luck.

He really had the monk now did Shoes... as he cast off his fourth feeder to a resounding crack. To my left two favoured pegs were neck and neck with six apiece. I couldn't have cared less because my battle was with peg five.

With ten minutes to go I had another dog of 3 lb plus. Complete silence now from Shoes. At the weigh-in my four bream and a few bits went 14 lb 5 oz which gave me fifth.

A late burst by Stu Killen put him top with 30lb. Trev was second with 25½ lb and Ade 'Bum Info' Seddon was third with a 22¼ lb net of roach.

For the record, Shoes is Simon Roffe, a Peterborough exile. His name comes from his job as a shoe shop manager. A nice lad and an up-and-coming angler.

ACTION REPLAY

ROACH AMO RAINBOWS

The Action Replay feature in Angler's Mail remains the most popular series in fishing. Nobody ever knows where our photographers are going to turn up next and that's half the fun of it! Here's a selection from our Replay files...

ENGLAND squad member Richard Borley (right) and London tackle dealer John Rose meet up with our Action Replay cameras at 8.30am on the banks of Ardleigh Reservoir in Essex.

Highly rated as a trout fishery, Ardleigh has also become recognised as one of the finest trout venues in Britain. The western narrows can be coarse fished from June and the whole water is thrown open to any method fishing from October onwards.

JOHN ROSE: I had 60lb of roach from this area last week and today looks perfect for an Action Replay. The weather's warm, there's hardly any breeze and there are some clouds to hide the sun — lovely! I caught well on waggler last time, so I've tackled up with my favourite 12ft Daiwa Matchlite rod, and ABU 602 closed face reel and a big waggler.

As I'm going to be fishing about three rods out, I've gone for a 3AAA bodied waggler with most of the shot bulked around the float. I shall be fishing on the drop, so I've strung out the rest of the shot shirt-button style with a No. 8 nearest the hook, then another ten inches away. Above that is a No. 6 and then finally a No. 4. That should give my bait a nice gentle fall through the water— just the way the roach like it.

NG THE

JR: Roach fishing at Ardleigh means casters, both on the hook and for feed. You need a lot, and I've brought four pints with me. You also need a lot of groundbait because the fish get through it very quickly, there's so many of them. I've got 12 lb of mixed brown and white groundbait, plus four pints of hemp.

I mix the casters and hemp in the groundbait and keep back some of the casters for hookbait and loose-feed. To attract the fish and keep them interested, I throw a sausage-shaped helping of groundbait in every cast. I then cast directly on top of the 'hole' the groundbait made, so that my hookbait is always falling through a cloud of feed and I'm always in with a chance of a bite.

Hookbait is single or double caster on a size 18 fine-wire barbless Drennan caster hook tied to 1.7 lb Bayer line.

RICHARD BORLEY: A week ago I had a 40 lb catch of roach in just three hours from this swim, and most of the fish were around the 1 lb mark. But there was more ripple on the water then, and I think that's an important factor, so I'm not sure how to go about it.

I fancy the pole today, and I've tackled up with a 12 metre Garbolino Turbo boron model, which has elestic running through the top two sections. My main line is 2 lb Maxima, tied to a 1.7 lb Bayer hook-length with a size 18 carbon Drennan caster hook at the business end. The float is an all balsa Milo pole float carrying a No. 8 Olivette and a No. 8 shot to dot it down.

If I can't catch on the pole, I intend to try further out with a big waggler or even the feeder. Long range fishing always seems to work well at Ardleigh, especially if it has been hard-fished.

RB: I agree with John that you need a lot of feed for the Ardleigh roach. I've brought three pints of hemp, three pints of casters and about 10lb of groundbait, which sounds a lot, but I don't expect to take any home.

I've plumbed the depth before starting to fish, and it's six feet deep on the 12 metre pole line, which is ideal. That's where I'll start my first attack, putting in three or four good sized balls of bait, with the casters and hemp mixed in, on the pole line.

I'm more confident now because a slight breeze has sprung up ruffling the surface of the water, which I'm sure makes the fish more confident. I'll keep topping up the swim with a golf-ball sized ball of groundbait every couple of minutes depending on the bites.

JR: I threw in three balls of groundbait while I was tackling up to give the swim time to settle, and now I'm ready to start. First cast to the baited area and I get a bite straight away from an 8 oz roach which I net, just to be on the safe side. Now I know the fish are in front of me, I try to develop a rhythm of groundbait, cast, strike and land fish, recast and groundbait again, until I'm doing everything automatically.

I find it helps me if I stand up, as it gives me greater control over my tackle and it's easier to get into a rhythm than if you are sitting down. Several more roach follow, all good ones around the 8-10 oz mark, then I get a fish that feels a bit different. It takes me a couple of minutes to land and proves to be a 1 lb trout which I put straight back.

RB: On my first cast I hook what turns out to be the best roach of the day, a lovely 1 lb 6 oz fish, which takes me a couple of minutes to land. There are no problems with the elastic doing its job perfectly and cushioning the line against the fish's lunges.

I start to catch steadily, nice roach of 6 to 10 oz with the odd fish over 1 lb but then like John, I start to have problems with the trout. The swim seems to be full of them and they intercept the bait before it can get down to the roach. At one stage I take nearly five trout in five casts, and the biggest at over 2½ lb takes me nearly five minutes to land on my matchfishing gear.

The only way to beat them is to change to a float taking a heavier Olivette, but even that makes no difference. The rules says that all trout have to be released immediately but that changes in October when for the price of a day ticket you can take eight trout home and still catch as many roach as you like.

JR: The trout have become a real problem in my swim as well as Richard's and they are taking the bait on the drop, before the roach have a chance. I'm going to try fishing deeper, with at least ten inches of line laid on the bottom. I moved my shot right down the line and set the float so that two No. 4's are just inches off the bottom and two No. 8s are lying hard on the bottom.

This has the effect of making the bites much slower and I have to wait for quite long intervals between them. But when they do come they are from roach not trout. I don't bother to net my fish now. I just slide them to hand and lift them out, which is another advantage of standing up in the water.

RB: I'm getting a bit fed up with catching trout — I must have had nearly 30 of them by now. So I'm going to try further out on the waggler. I'll try loose-feeding to start with and fish with a three swan waggler to give me the range. But first I'll put in three balls of groundbait on the 30 yard line and give it a couple of minutes to settle down.

As soon as I cast out, I get a good roach and for 30 minutes it's a bite a chuck with good roach, and a bonus perch of 1½ lb, all taken on double caster. The perch is a bit of a surprise though I know there are some good ones in Ardleigh. After a while the long range swim dies, so I go back on the pole and luckily the trout seem to have gone because I catch a steady stream of roach to 1lb before packing up at 2.30pm.

RB: At the end of the session I've 22 lb of roach in the net, comprising 40 fish averaging 8-10 oz plus the 1½ lb perch and about 30 trout which together must have weighed well over 30 lb. At what other water can you catch 20 lb of roach from every peg? Ardleigh must rate as one of the best roach fisheries in the country and I can't wait until we start holding matches here in late October and early November.

JR: I finished with about 15 lb of roach and 20 lb of trout which wasn't as good as I hoped. I really had to work hard to catch fish but when I had 60 lb last week it was a roach a cast from the first chuck to the last. But I love fishing this water, it's so consistent with the chance of a good catch from every swim. And there's always the opportunity of a big fish as well.

ACTION REPLAY

DAZZLER FROM A DEEP HOLE

THE River Cherwell in Oxfordshire is classic chub territory. And who better to join for a day's fishing than Terry Brindle, secretary of the Chub Study Group.

This length of the Cherwell is owned by Kidlington AS who issue a limited number of day-tickets through Mill Street Pets in Kidlington. It's very popular with match anglers and I always check beforehand to make sure there's not a contest booked. The chub don't run big, a 4 lb fish is a very good one, and five-pounders are relatively rare. But what it lacks in size, this river makes up for in quantity. On a good day I'd expect a couple of three's in a bag of five or six fish but I'm not very confident this morning. There was a heavy frost last night and the temperature now is only just above freezing point. But on the plus side, it has been very cold for nearly a fortnight so the fish should be used to it and the river looks good, with a nice colour and flow.

Cheese paste made from Danish Blue tops my list of winter chub baits. It is a good attractor because of the smell and if you mix it correctly it doesn't go hard in cold water. I make mine from ½ lb of grated Cheddar and half a white loaf. You must allow the bread to go stale for a couple of days before mixing up a soft breadpaste. Remember your hands must be clean when doing this otherwise the bread becomes tainted. I add the cheese gradually to the bread until I have about 1½ lb of cheese paste, enough for a session. To increase its attractiveness I add a couple of 5 ml spoons of Terry Eustace Blue Cheese essence. I'm convinced it makes a difference to my catches. I also take breadflake and a few worms with me. But I'm struggling if the cheesepaste doesn't work.

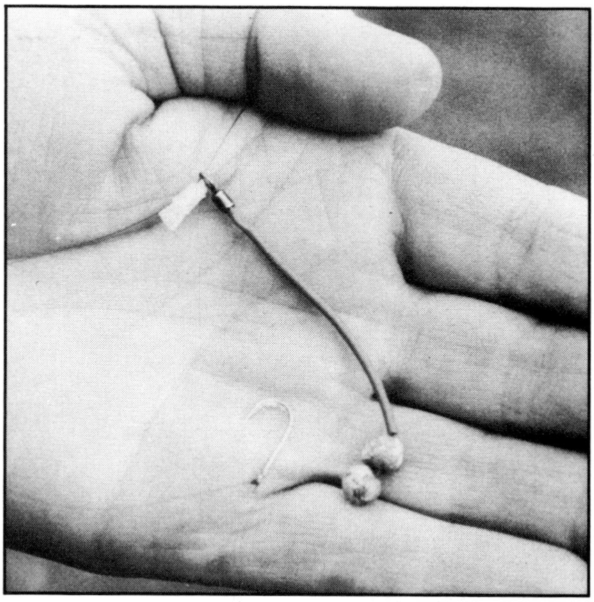

Most of my chub are caught from under my feet which demands a stealthy approach. For that reason I keep my gear to a minimum, with just a rod, reel, a few shot, hooks and other odds and ends, plus a landing net. The rod is a 1¼ lb test curve, through-action carp model made from a North Western blank, about ten years old. I normally twin it with a Mitchell 300 loaded with 5 lb Maxima line. I've been trying Drennan carbon specimen hooks and so far have no complaints. They are strong and very sharp and don't lose their point. My terminal tackle is a simple link leger, though I like to have a 2 in. length of silicone tubing on my link to prevent tangling. The leger stop I make at home from a Biro tube. A couple of swanshot are all the weight I need as I won't be fishing at any range. For detecting bites I use a screwed in 9in., 1½ oz. quivertip which is soft enough to show the most delicate of bites.

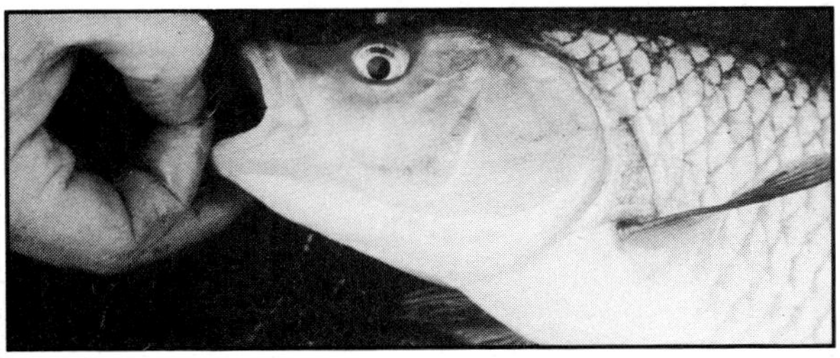

I'm ready to start fishing now, but first I walk the stretch, throwing in a few knobs of cheesepaste into all the likely looking swims. All the usual spots are covered — rafts of debris, undercut banks, deeper holes, and bends where the river has scoured a deeper area. I watch where the current takes the bait, making mental notes to try each spot, before walking back to the start of the venue to start fishing. The first swim I try is a sweeping bend where the main flow is on the far side of the river and there is a dead tree in the water. On the halfway mark is a crease in the flow and that's where I cast a large piece of paste on a size 6 hook. After 10 minutes, I try twitching the bait. On the second or third twitch my tip belts round and the first fish of the day, a 3 lb 7 oz chub, comes to the net. An excellent start — I rate any chub over 3 lb a good 'un.

After catching the 3 lb 7 oz fish I throw in a couple of pieces of bait and then move on to the next swim, intending to return later if there's time. The new swim has a line of hawthorns on my bank with a raft of rubbish downstream. I flick out a bait and let the current roll it under the raft. Within five minutes the tip goes round and a 2 lb 13 oz chub comes out. I held it hard on the 5 lb line and just eased it away from the raft and out of danger. It was on the bank within a minute but I'm very pleased to have caught two good fish within such a short space of time. After this, I bait up the swim with more cheese, and move on to the next. But after trying a number of spots without response, I reach the end of the venue and decide to work my way back up again.

I walk along to a swim which I didn't try earlier because there were a number of swans in it, stirring up the bottom. It's quite a difficult pitch — there's a long run of hawthorns and brambles on the near bank which ends suddenly in a deep hole. To approach it I crawl on hands and knees up to the river's edge and then poke the rod tip over the edge of the bank, dropping my bait down into the hole. It settled on the bottom, I tightened up, and the quivertip pulled over almost in the same instant. As soon as I hit the fish I knew it was a good 'un, It ran halfway across the river and put up a very spirited fight for two or three minutes before I slid the net under a 4¼ lb chub, my best to date from this stretch. My best from the Cherwell of 4 lb 14 oz came from another length. It was a lovely short, fat bronze specimen that I was absolutely delighted to catch.

After the excitement of the four-pounder everything went quiet. I went virtually the whole afternoon without another bite, despite trying every baited swim, and offering breadlflake as well as paste. It became steadily colder and by dusk it must have been several degrees below freezing. I started to think of packing up but decided on a last cast at 4pm in the swim that produced the 4¼ lb chub. Within five minutes I had a bite and landed a 2 lb 6 oz chub. Spurred on by this action, I tried another swim at the top of the venue, near where I started to see if my luck had changed. This swim is a classic with a raft of rubbish and sure enough I took another of 3 lb 14 oz from underneath it, just as it was getting dark and before deciding that enough was enough.

I'm more than pleased with my final tally of five chub, topped by a personal best for the stretch of 4¼ lb. I only missed one half-bite all day which was satisfying, as I don't like missing bites. I was very apprehensive about fishing for the camera, especially as I had tried this stretch the previous weekend with a pal, and in ten hours' fishing we didn't get a single bite between us! So I was delighted it came off, especially as the weather was so cold. These chub are the 4¼ lb, the 3 lb 7 oz and 2 lb 13 oz fish — the others I caught right at the end of the day when the light had gone and I put them straight back. The Chub Study Group logs all chub over 4 lb, so I shall definitely enter my best fish, as a way of recording the state of our rivers. Unfortunately, most seem to be declining, but I think today shows that good catches can still be made with a little effort and thought.

ACTION REPLAY

Battle of wits on the Wharfe

YOU'VE got to take the conditions as you find them in fishing — and on Yorkshire rivers that frequently represents a real challenge. But there's no better angler to pick up the gauntlet than Leeds ace HOWARD ROBSON whose impressive career has included appearances for England. We asked him to get the best from the River Wharfe day ticket waters in North Yorkshire controlled by Boston Spa AA.

This is one of my favourite swims on the two-mile length of the Wharfe and is close to the village of Newton Kyme, near Tadcaster, at the bottom of the stretch.

Catches of over 30 lb of chub and barbel are frequently taken on this fishery, including individual fish up to 5 lb, although larger barbel occasionally show.

The river is carrying 18 inches of extra water, but is reasonably clear. It is now midday and the light is murky. There is promise of a sunny afternoon, so let's get started, as our chances of catching good fish will not be enhanced by the appearance of the sun.

For this afternoon session I've brought along two pints of casters, lucheon meat and some waspgrub. Any of these baits, of course, are suitable for chub and barbel, but if the larger fish are not co-operating I may be able to pick up some dace on floatfished caster.

Waspgrub can be very good bait at this time of year, especially for chub, but collecting wasps' nests is not everyone's idea of fun and should be avoided unless you really know your stuff!

For those who prefer more easily obtained baits, luncheon meat is just as good an alternative and I occasionally use breadflake with success.

My intention is to start with a legered bait close to the submerged trees across the river. The rod I am using for this is a Lee's Aquaglass which is some 25 years old. It was originally a 12ft bottom rod but when a bullock made short work of the top section some years ago, I fitted a new top length, hand carved with a knife to form a quivertip and fitted an agate ring from a 1910 greenheart fly rod. The rod is now 10ft long.

I prefer to use a fixed spool reel for casting long distances, and this one is a Sundridge Skorpio.

I like to keep my terminal tackle simple. The reel line is 4 lb Sylcast monofilament and the hook length is 3 lb.

I am using a ½oz Arlesey bomb, on a short swivel-link, stopped with a single No. 4 shot, 18 inches from a size 6 Mustad Sproat hook. After one or two exploratory casts, I find that there is sufficient weight just to hold the bottom near the snags. I have chosen a large hook suitable for meat, waspgrub or a combination of the two.

It has been impossible to get bites anywhere in the swim except within two yards of the large, partly submerged tree trunk which means a cast of some 25-30 yards. With the extra water in the river, the depth at this point is around 6ft, with about 10ft in the centre.

The bites I've had have been very tentative and hard concentration has been essential to convert these bites to fish in the net. After fishing for about two hours, however, I have landed six chub of between 1 and 2 lb, all taken on luncheon meat.

As forecast, the mist and cloud have now disappeared and the sun is shining quite strongly.

There was a lot of rain in the Pennine hills a few days ago when temperatures were low and this cold water is now finding its way into the river here. The tentative bites I have been getting have become even more cautious and certainly less frequent.

I have been careful not to overfeed in these conditions, loose feeding small amounts of casters with the occasional piece of meat.

After waiting for an hour, biteless, there is a sudden twitch at the end of the quivertip and after a brief surge towards the snags, I land a nice chub.

This chub, in the 2½-3 lb range, is the best fish of the session so far and again came from the same spot near the trees, falling for meat/waspcake cocktail.

The fish seem reluctant to leave this area and I still can't get bites anywhere else in the swim.

I am really having to put my thinking cap on now, ringing the changes with baits, and I'll try the swimfeeder although, in conditions like today's, I fear that the noise of the feeder entering the water may put the fish off.

It's now 4pm and in the last hour only one more fish has shown interest in the meat-baited hook and joined its fellows in the keepnet — a chub of similar size to the last one — making a total of eight fish, all chub.

No barbel have shown and I am sure that the sudden drop in temperature is the reason for this.

I'm struggling now, having tried the feeder with no success and I've had a spell of swimming a 3½ swan stick float down the middle, but I can't keep the float tackle near the snags because the flow is too strong, so back to the bomb.

With the sun fast approaching the horizon, it's time to end the session. I have added another small chub to the catch making a total of nine fish, all chub weighing 13½ lb in total.

The best two fish of the day were about 3½ lb each and although I am disappointed not to have had some barbel, it is satisfying to have caught a few fish on a day when conditions were not good and other anglers fishing nearby were struggling to catch any fish at all.

ACTION REPLAY

FUN-FISHING FOR PIKE

NORWICH tackle dealer John Wilson takes us pike fishing on Rockland Broad in Norfolk where the fish don't run big but light tackle produces some lively action.

With a very limited amount of bank space available, Rockland Broad is best fished from a boat and I've brought with me all the equipment I would use when fishing for pike. That means four rods — two for livebaiting, one for deadbaiting and one for plug fishing, though I'll only be using two at a time to comply with Water Authority byelaws.

Then there's my livebait bucket, two large carry-alls full of odds and ends like waterproof clothing, and a 42-inch landing net, though I prefer to land my fish by hand. Two home-made concrete anchors and a pair of oars complete the list. So let's load up the boat and get cracking.

Boats are not available for hire at Rockland and I've borrowed this one from a friend, as there are no restrictions on anglers bringing their own boats. Contact Mr Dye on Surlingham 256 beforehand, because he controls the launching slipway and there is a small charge for launching your boat.

Rockland is full of pike, ranging from jacks to fish in the upper double figures and that make for fun fishing. Rarely have the fish let me down and a good day can produce a dozen pike, half of them doubles.

I'm heading for the deeper north-western corner of the broad where there is six to ten feet of water which acts as a natural holding area.

I've arrived at my chosen pitch, a deep channel between two banks of reeds and dropped anchor — it's time to tackle up. For livebaiting I use two 1¼ lb test curve North Western Avon blanks twinned with Mitchell 308 reels, loaded with 6 lb Sylcast line. I'm not expecting to catch monster pike, so 6 lb should be more than adequate.

I tie a 20 in. 15 lb trace to the line using a single swanshot as the weight under a one-inch pilot float stopped with an inch of peacock quill. A float of this size is sufficient to cope with the small livebaits I use. I'm not keen on the majority of pike floats because quite simply they are too big and bulky.

For livebaits, I prefer small roach and rudd of about 2 oz. or about five inches long. I don't believe in using anything larger because bigger fish represent the size of fish many anglers like to catch and if anything we have been over-preserving pike at the expense of other fish. Also, small baits make unhooking pike much easier and they are less likely to come unstuck.

I keep my baits in an ET livebait grill within my bait bucket, and take this out and hang it over the side of the boat when anchored up. This ensures that the fish are in freshwater all the time. An aerator keeps them alive when they are in the bucket.

After the nine-pounder, I took a fish of 5 lb, again on a livebait, then another of about 4 lb on the Big S plug. I tried wobbling a deadbait on the long rod and had a couple of runs but each time the fish dropped the bait for some reason before I could strike.

After a while, I went back to the livebait rods and within minutes had another run from this fish which feels a bit better than the rest. It suddenly comes to the surface in a tail-walking flurry of spray — something they tend to do more in the summer than in winter. Rockland pike fight all the same way — non-stop, like they're trying to pull your arm out of its socket.

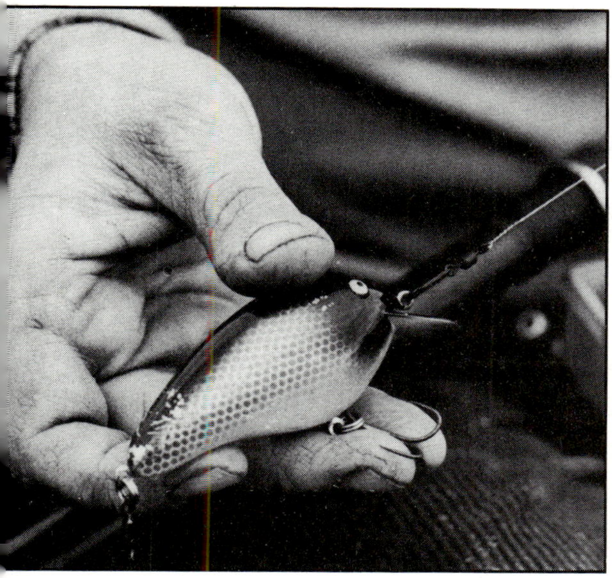

After setting up my two livebait rods, I tackle up my deadbait rod, an 11ft North Western blank with a 1¾ lb test curve. This is coupled with a Mitchell 300 reel loaded with 11lb Sylcast line which is about the heaviest I use in pike fishing. My other rod is an old 8ft hollow glass plugging rod, again loaded with 11 lb line on a Mitchell 300.

The plug I'm going to use today is a Big S type which I rate as the most versatile model you can use. It floats when you don't wind it in, and sinks when you do, and it has an adjustable diving vane on the front which allows you to fish as deep as you want simply by altering the angle. I sold one to Paul Kerry recently and he landed a 25 lb pike on it, first cast!

This is the first fish of the day, a nine-pounder which fell to small roach livebait. It fought with the typical fight of a Rockland pike and took me several minutes to boat. I didn't bother with the net but lifted it straight out, unhooked it, and slid it back almost immediately — that way the minimum damage is caused to both fish and angler. That fish came to the fourth run of the day. I missed the first three by striking too early, I think.

The fish are finicky probably because of the low water temperature which is down in the mid-40's after the recent cold spell, though it's very mild today.

After several minutes I managed to control the fish, brought it alongside, and allowed it to quieten down. Then I put a leather gardening glove on my left hand and lifted out the fish by putting my hand inside the gill cover, well away from the delicate gill filaments. As I lift, I curl my left hand towards me which has the effect of opening the pike's lower jaw and giving me easy access to the small size 10 trebles I use. A quick twist with a pair of artery forceps and the fish is unhooked and ready to go straight back. For this sort of unhooking operation, the glove must be made of leather — the pike can quite easily bite through plastic.

This is my best fish of the day, at 11 lb a bit on the light side as Rockland doubles go but it fought well enough on the 6 lb line. I'm convinced that anglers could get more fun out of pike fishing by using lighter lines. They would quite readily use 6 lb line for large tench, barbel or even carp in some situations and a pike does not fight harder than any of those three.

It wasn't a particularly good day compared with some catches I've taken at Rockland but at least I didn't fail to catch and the beauty of the place is that it rarely lets me down.

TACKLE ON TEST

Expert assessment of all types of angling equipment costing from a few pence to many hundreds of pounds feature in the Mail's Tackle on Test columns. Here's a selection of our published reviews...

COMPACT OPTONICS

THE Optonic electronic bite indicator incorporates an ingenious system where the line runs over an ultra-light wheel.

When a fish takes line, the wheel revolves and turns a paddle which then interrupts a light beam activating a sounder. Drop back bites are also detected if the wheel turns backwards.

Efgeeco's updated versions of the original Optonics are the compact type which incorporate the sounder within the indicator head eliminating the need for an additional sounder box with leads.

A neat protective box is provided but these days many anglers leave their indicators on bank sticks and place cloth covers over them.

The Special Compact comes in high or low tone with a red flashing LED and a volume control which can be adjusted to alert just you and not the entire population of fishermen on the water.

At their loudest, both high and low tones will wake you up if you have nodded off during the session.

They also feature an on/off switch, which I found to be a bit fiddly, and jacket sockets so that you can connect an external sounder box if need be.

For example, you may like to place the sounder under your bedchair.

The Super Compact is the Rolls Royce of the range. It has all the features of the Special Compact but in addition it has tone control and latching LED.

I particularly liked the tone of this version when set on its deepest value. It is a mellow buzz and not a raucous screech that is the bane of people who like a bit of piece and quiet.

Latching LED's are very useful. This one stays on for about eight seconds after a bite which means that if you were not looking at your rods at the right moment you can hover over the right one waiting for it to develop.

This could mean the difference between hitting or not hitting the next twitch.

I found this new generation of Optonics worked without fault and so I would definitely recommend them.

ANDY ORME

MUSTAD 16650B BARBLESS HOOK

THE match angler has plenty of barbless hooks to choose from but there are precious few decent eyed patterns designed for larger fish like carp tench and barbel.

I was pleased, therefore, to receive a sample pack of the new Mustad barbless hooks, pattern No. 16650B.

The notes I received with the hooks described them as being based on the popular 1665 "boy's eyed hook" but this belies the quality.

When testing the hook's temper I found it to be as strong as most other hooks I have tried.

It is made from forged carbon steel and has a long shank, a neat eye and a sharp and offset point.

Of prime importance is the fact that they have a deep throat which I consider vital in barbless hooks.

The throat is the distance between the point and the bottom of the bend. Fish are more likely to roll off shallower round-bend hooks.

The point is sharp but in my opinion, too long and fine making it rather susceptible to losing its point easily should it strike a pebble or catch a branch.

I tried out the hooks on a morning session after tench. I will admit now to having a deep prejudice against barbless hooks, but not to be intimidated I used the hooks on both rods.

Fishing mini-boilies on hairs, tied from the eye of the hook, I awaited in trepidation for that first run and lost fish – but the result was nine hooked fish!

Five of the tench went over 5lb and all of them fought like Trojans.

I used a size 8, the largest in the range, but I wish the hook was available in sixes and fours as well.

The 16650B barbless is reasonably priced and certainly suited to the younger angler as well as the discerning specimen hunter.

KEVIN SMITH

DAIWA AUTOC

DAIWA'S Autocast reel is not entirely new to the market — but it is still a stranger to many seasoned anglers.

Like many others, I had heard of and seen the reel but never tried it. And when I first picked it up, I wasn't too enthralled by what felt like a bulky reel.

Although the reel felt big it is, in fact, exceptionally light, being made from graphite.

SHAKESPEARE PAN NET AND CARBON HANDLE

IF you're content to fish for what comes along then a circular landing net frame is out in front.

Not everybody will agree, but a round net gives a more balanced feeling in the hand. It also has a slight edge over rectangular models for manoeuvrability.

Yet nets remain a very personal matter. Some swear by round ones for fish of all sizes — while others maintain they're strictly for the small stuff.

Leaving that argument aside, the sheer popularity of match pan nets suggests that fish are spending considerably less time nowadays flapping in the meshing.

Speed of unhooking is significantly aided by models like Shakespeare's strongly constructed match pan net which comes in 20in. and 24in. sizes.

Couple it with the new Carbo telescopic landing net handle weighing just 12½oz and you've got one of the best combinations in its class.

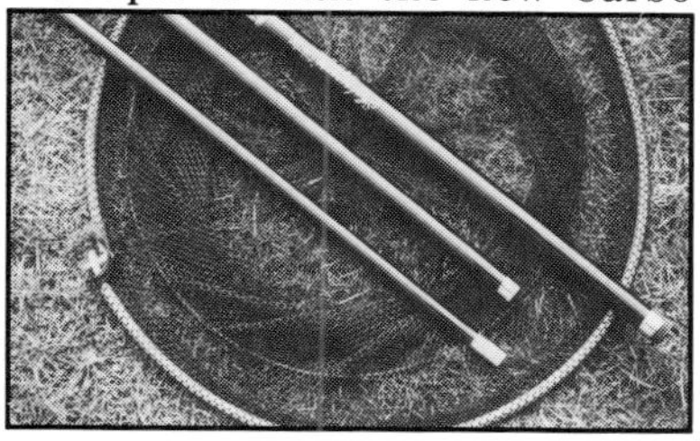

The telescopic handle will extend to 9½ ft if you need that much reach and the joints are protected with lightweight metal rings.

For most fishing you can dispense with the butt section leaving a very compact length that comes readily to hand.

ROY WESTWOOD

T REEL

My first few outings resulted in my virtually ignoring the Autocast facility and doing the work manually by lifting the bale arm as normal.

Eventually, as I came to realise just how good a reel the AG1655 was — light, smooth operating and with a nice "feel" while playing fish — I became adventurous and used the Autocast.

Basically, it is a lever positioned next to the roller on the bale arm which is pulled back with the forefinger to open the bale.

Clever design ensures the trigger and line are where you want them — handy for the finger every time you wish to cast.

All you do is engage the anti-reverse and a back turn of the handle ensures the lever is where you need it for casting. Casting is also simple once you have become confident enough to use the facility.

The anti-reverse switch, stern drag, left or right wind and a quick change spool facility, along with deep and shallow spools, make this a great reel.

COLIN MITCHELL

ABU AMBASSADEUR 6500GR

IT is the basic rule of setting the spool drag on a casting multiplier that the greater the wind resistance, the more heavily the reel must be dampened.

In practical terms, this means that if you cast a single bait neatly clipped down, it will need less braking on the spool to prevent an over-run than if you had three baits and were belting it into a headwind.

Braking requirements can vary considerably during a fishing session because of variations in terminal tackle so, it's a godsend to have a multiplier where the spool braking it variable by the simple movement of a calibrated button.

This is the outstanding feature of the Abu 6500GR, and the lever is mounted on top of the reel and can even be adjusted in flight if necessary.

Metal is out for sideplates and graphite composite in, which means an end to that perennial problem of corrosion.

Inevitably, the reel will have to have its levelwind mechanism removed if big distances are wanted, but existing Abu conversion kits are almost certain to fit the GR.

I just wish a levelwind-less version was available as standard.

BOB GLEDHILL

The slim, neat tube joint between fly line and braid. This is the dry fly leader made from twisted nylon.

REVOLUTION BRAIDED LEADERS

YOU can improve your casting performance by switching to a supple braided leader.

That's the bold claim of Ryobi Masterline who market a range of Revolution tapered leaders in five different densities.

The 9ft long braided leaders include a length of mono at the business end to which you attach a tippet of the required strength.

Joining the hollow braid to the fly line itself takes a matter of seconds. I was surprised at the ease of the operation and even more taken aback by the security of it all.

All you do is feed the end of the fly line into the open braid at the butt end of the leader and slide a length of plastic tubing over the join (see diagram).

Everything's supplied and leaders can be switched very quickly at the water-side.

A similarity in suppleness between a braided leader and the fly line produces a more continuous flow of energy during casting.

Improved distance, accuracy, turn-over and presentation are claimed for these leaders which are sold in dry, neutral density, sinking, fast sinking and heavyweight categories.

The dry fly leader is made from twisted nylon instead of braid to help absorb the stresses of smash takes.

As a user of 15 lb butts and level 7 lb leaders, I'm reluctant to change to a system which offers even a hint of a weak link.

But after abusing these braided leaders and tube connectors and pulling for a break against a dead weight, I've decided they'll more than withstand my lack of finesse on lakes.

ROY WESTWOOD

Attaching a Revolution Braided Leader to a fly line.

1. Push end of fly line into open braid at the butt end of leader and thread it through for about an inch.

2. Cut off length of plastic tubing, about ¾in, and thread it on other end of leader.

3. Run tubing all way along to where fly line enters braided monofil and ease it over the connection so that the end of the braid is midway under the tube.

Instructions courtesy of Ryobi Masterline

TACKLE ON TEST

Rigid all the way... no bend at 11 metres in the Carboron.

DAM Carboron Pole

The Carboron 12 metre pole became a firm favourite of mine — even before I had fished with it!

Like most other top-class items of tackle, I knew instantly from the feel of the pole that it was right for the job. High praise from my old friend Ian Heaps, the former World Champion, was well placed.

At the time I was struggling to hold a ten metre pole which I found too heavy. The Carboron at 9½ metres could be held in one hand.

The extension pieces put the Carboron to 10½, 11 or 12 metres. It remains remarkably rigid at all these lengths, doesn't go sloppy and is light enough to fish a full five hour match with (as long as you use two hands!).

The whole of the pole is black with the top three sections telescopic and the rest takes apart. The lower, thicker sections fit into the upper ones.

I had to cut off around six inches from the hollow tip to take the fitting for my internal elastic but that trimming still meant the tip was just the right thickness for the business end.

If you go wrong cutting back there is always the spare tip to start on — although that can best be cut back a few inches to insert a fine flick tip from the inside. It could also be used for a spare, elastic carrying tip.

I've landed chub to 2½ lb on the pole, on 12 oz bottoms and fine wire 22 hooks. The internal elastic came out perfectly for the big fish and the amount of power in the top sections of the pole was just right to beat the fish fairly quickly without hauling it through the water.

Small fish can easily be bounced off on long poles, but I have yet to have this happen with the Carboron because it does not flop around heavily as you unship sections.

The one criticism I do have is that the ferrules could have been smoothed down better so they don't catch your hands as you feed it back to unship.

You may find a lighter pole, you may get a thinner butt section. But I should think you will find it hard to better this pole at the price.

COLIN MITCHELL

DEPTHOMETER

THE Depthometer is a handy little gadget for checking the depth of your swim from a range of one yard to 100.

It is basically a glass tube calibrated with depths from 5ft to 80ft which you can cast into your chosen swim after tying it onto the end of the line, and allowing it to sink to the bottom.

Waters enters through a brass fitting at the base of the tube and is forced under pressure up the tube to the depth of the swim.

The next bit is important – the Depthometer should now be retrieved at a steady rate, not allowing it to rise and then fall again as this produces false readings.

When you've retrieved it hold the Depthometer upright and measure the level of water inside against the calibrations on the side of the tube to get an accurate reading of the depth of your swim.

To re-set the device for your next cast simply unscrew the brass fitting in the base to release the water and you're ready to go again.

I tested the Depthometer on a gravel pit swim I know intimately and found it accurate to within a foot or so though I did have problems locating a slight dip in the lake-bed which is a noted hotspot in this swim.

The beauty of this little device lies in the ease with which it can be used. To check the depth beneath an overhanging bush or to gain an overall impression of a swim's depth there is little to fault it.

KEVIN SMITH

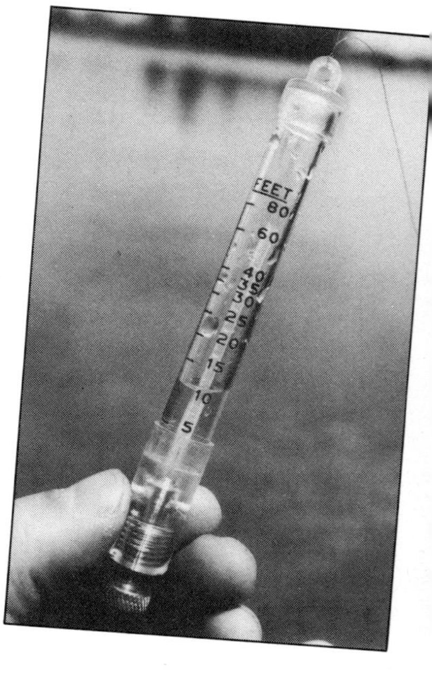

Fast worker!

Coventry specimen hunter Phil Smith captured this superb 13lb 7oz bream from Oxfordshire's Queenford Lagoon.

Regulars expect to go days on this water without a bite but Phil hooked the 13-pounder and another huge bream of 15lb 3oz within hours of starting a 14-day session.

Both fish fell to lobworms legered on a specially cleared gravel bar in this thickly weeded Lagoon. Phil used a small rowing boat to clear and bait his swim.

PICTURE: PHIL SMITH

That's different!

There's no apparent connection with this angler fishing on the Hampshire Avon near Salisbury and the land of cuckoo clocks and Nestles chocolate. But Roy Buckland hooked this 1½lb grayling on a bee grub specially imported from Switzerland.

Roy, from Salisbury, was fishing below the town on the Britford stretch and rates the rare grub as the No. 1 bait for grayling, catching a netful on an autumn afternoon to prove his point.

PICTURE: TREVOR HOUSBY

Catfish fishing requires enormous patience as the species often go for days without feeding.

But there's no-one better at playing the waiting game than Catfish Conservation Group secretary Bob Baldock seen here with a 11lb specimen from Claydon Lake in Bedfordshire.

Even small cats fight like demons and Bob had his hands full controlling the fish on 9lb line and a powerful 1¾lb test curve rod.

PO
HEAVY

EVEN by today's standards of hefty average weights in trout fishing, Willow Pool is exceptional.

The Oxford water regularly produces double-figure specimens and there's a generous stocking with fish over 4lb.

Bruce Vaughan, marketing manager of Ryobi Masterline, gets to grips here with a 5lb rainbow from the favoured deep water bank near the fishing lodge.

He used a nymph tied by Gloucestershire dresser Dave Tait which incorporates a weighted head specially imported from the States.

Willow Pool forms part of the ARC managed Linch Hill fishery at Stanton Harcourt.

L OF
VEIGHTS

An early season angler slugs it out with a battling tench on Lincolnshire's Grantham Canal, one of the county's most improved waters.

Tench catches approaching three-figures are not unknown at the start of the season from the narrow waterway and there are plenty of big bream to be caught if pulling out tench loses its appeal.

PICTURE: RODNEY COLDRON

Carp in Devon must have strange taste buds — this 15lb leather showed a liking for a spearmint flavoured boilie!

It was the fish of a lifetime for 15-year-old Nicky Barrett from Ilford in Essex who caught it while on holiday at Paradise lakes, Halwill in mid Devon. The young angler had a 15-minute struggle with the specimen on 8lb line.

PICTURE: MIKE MILLMAN

North East matchman Ken Close is a real ace with waspgrub baits and that's how he collected this 20lb net of chub from a favourite stretch of the River Tees at Croft where the fish proved suckers for two grubs trotted under far bank willows.

To prove that it was the bait which made the difference, Ken switched to fishing with casters for an hour and caught only small fish. Back on with the grub and another 2lb-plus chub came splashing to the net.

At the end of a four hour session, Ken had ten chub to 2lb 9oz, plus some smaller fish in his net, showing why he was voted North East Match Angler of the Year twice in succession.

PICTURE: DENNIS LINLEY

THE BAIT REVOLUTION

Now there's colours and flavours to suit every swim and species, reports DAVE COSTER

BAIT selection has become rather more complicated since the development of numerous colour and flavour combinations both for the most basic of baits like maggots and for groundbaits.

In fact, there's been a virtual revolution in the thinking and preparation that goes into the baits anglers carry to the waterside.

It would probably be fair to say much of this change in attitude has come about through the modern carp and specimen angler's preoccupation with attractors and stimulators.

THE BAIT REVOLUTION

With records tumbling regularly over the past few years in big fish circles, it was inevitable that other coarse anglers would want to share in this new found success.

Over the past two or three years, coarse fishing generally has followed a trend of seeking to develop ways of making basic baits more attractive.

Phrases like 'pulling power' and 'holding power' are commonly used and the days of simply purchasing half-a-pint of white maggots and a pound of plain breadcrumbs seem long gone.

Indeed, there is little incentive to opt for bland basic ingredients when most tackle shops now offer such extensive ranges of flavourings, colourings and different types of bait.

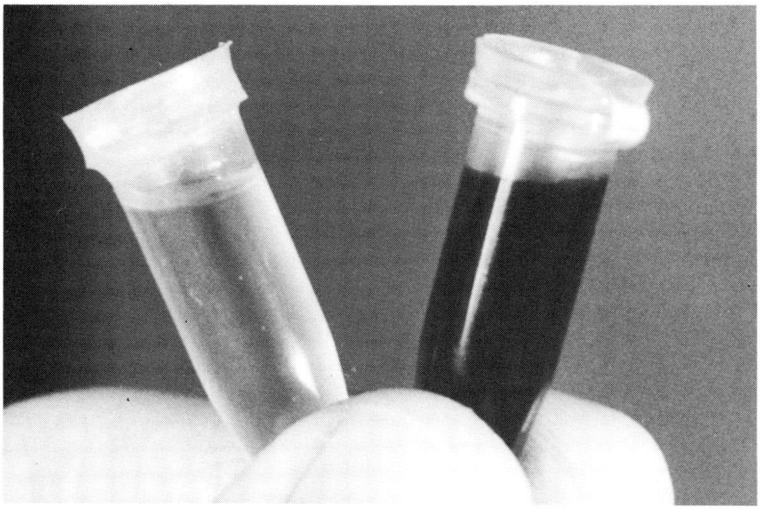

Phials of flavour for maggots — a treatment that's really caught on.

COLOURING

IT is true that fish respond better to certain colours than others. Whether this is do with visibility or attractiveness is a mute point.

Most probably by colouring baits, an angler is making an offering more natural looking from the fish's viewpoint. But, there is always the possibility that on waters where red, yellow or bronze maggots dominate catches, their popularity survives simply because that is the colour the fish are constantly weaned onto!

Whatever the reason, hookbait colour can be very important. Seasoned matchmen will vouch for this and the novice could well improve his catches by seeking hard information on this score when setting out to fish a new water.

There are, of course, basic rules worth looking at with coloured hookbaits. Tench and bream particularly seem to favour red maggots or pinkies. This is very likely because these fish grub around on the bottom and a red maggot must resemble bloodworm or an earthworm.

Perch also will accept red maggots when nothing else in the maggot spectrum will tempt them. A final point worth mentioning on the subject of reds is its ability to draw attention in coloured water.

On flooded rivers and coloured canals it can be deadly, which tends to back up the theory that red is more visible in such conditions.

Bronze maggots were developed during the caster boom and have stayed popular ever since. Anglers often found that feeding casters and fishing a bronze maggot on the hook, produced many more bites.

This was probably because a maggot gave movement to the hookbait and made the offering stand out against the inert caster loose-feed.

But anglers later found that bronze maggots fed in heavy quantities would account for some outstanding roach and chub catches and this is still the case today.

Yellow hookbaits are something of a tradition on some venues and always seem to work best in conjunction with a similarly coloured groundbait.

Skimmer bream, roach and dace show a liking for this colour at times and it is interesting that carp anglers often favour yellow boilies.

Of course, one of the most popular baits of recent years falls into this category and that is sweetcorn. It's a superb carp and tench bait, but even the humble corn has come in for the colouring treatment and some superb catches have resulted with red dyed sweetcorn.

The first intensive experiments with bait flavours occured in carp fishing and now there's a massive range of attractors available over the counter.

GROUNDBAITS

COLOURATION would also appear to be an important factor in groundbaits. Continental mixes are very popular in this country and range in shades from almost white, through to dark greys and browns and from reds to yellows.

Lighter groundbaits are more successfully employed for surface and on-the-drop styles of fishing, while darker groundbaits are better suited for bottom presentation.

Some of the best selling Continental brands carry up to 20 different ingredients and with the high level of expertise shown by top Continental pole anglers, it would be a very brave angler who ignored their impressive array of mixes.

The Continentals rely very much on feeding large amounts of groundbait into their swims. They vary the consistencies dramatically so that the feed breaks down at different intervals to disperse free offerings like bloodworm and jokers into the water.

We have applied Continental mixes somewhat differently in this country, mainly because our competitions last a lot longer than those of our friends across the Channel. But their mixes have still proved effective.

Popular ingredients used as attractors are hemp, breadcrumbs, biscuit flour, maize, mollasses, pigeon droppings, dried blood, coconut, walnut flour, poppy seeds — the list is endless. But it has made us think more deeply about what we feed into our swims.

FLAVOURINGS

AFTER experimenting with Continental mixes most anglers do find they pull more fish and they certainly have more holding qualities than basic breadcrumb feeds.

This has led to English anglers tarting up breadcrumbs with liquid flavourings and some interesting results have followed.

In warm summer months, sweet flavourings like maple, vanilla and sweetcorn are very successful, but as the weather turns colder more savoury offerings like cheese, luncheon meat and a host of 'naturals' like freshwater mussel, crayfish and worm extract take over.

Success at this level has spread into flavouring the hookbait and loose offerings also.

Currently it is possible to purchase flavours specially designed for use with maggots and casters. The angler can buy a small phial of flavouring to add to his bait the evening before a fishing trip or actually on the bank.

These flavours range from being all-purpose to special aromas designed with certain species in mind.

Generally, the sweeter flavourings tend to be aimed at fish like roach, bream and carp, while savoury blends are popular for fish like chub and barbel.

The most comprehensive ranges of flavourings are still of course produced with the carp angler in mind, but the average coarse angler can carry his research into this area for his needs.

The only thing to remember is that most carp orientated liquid flavours are highly concentrated and it is possible to over saturate baits and groundbaits to the point where they become too potent.

With experience, most anglers find lesser quantities of additives are needed when the fish are active in warm weather, while doses can be stepped up quite dramatically in colder winter months in the quest for positive takes.

Undoubtedly, a bait revolution is upon us. So if your catch rates are constantly low, or the anglers around you always seem to be streets ahead, why not give flavourings a try?

Continental groundbaits can also improve your catches. Failing that, you can alway develop your own special mixes. The ingredients are now readily available and you never know you may stumble on a winning formula!

Plain brown crumb can be revitalised with a handful of one of the many continental mixtures.

LONELINESS OF THE LONG DISTANCE WRECKERS

MIKE MILLMAN on the dedicated deep sea anglers who seek the finest fishing in the world — over the horizon

Spoils of mid-channel wrecking. A 23lb turbot taken on mackerel when the boat swung off the main part of the hulk. Many turbot hide out in sandy hollows around the hull.

TO every point of the compass there was nothing but heaving water. A force five wind blowing diagonally against the running tide was creating deep troughs and the 38ft long charter boat rose a dozen feet then slipped down the steep incline as the swell moved on, only to be replaced by another.

The anchor rope which entered the water a good 20ft from the bows, slapped the sea noisily as it strained to hold the 5½ ton Artilleryman II in a precise position.

Several hundred feet behind the boat and 44 fathoms below the surface was a wreck of considerable size. It had been on the bottom for 40 years and long forgotten until a sophisticated echo-sounder steadily plotting the bottom configuration as a matter of routine searching had revealed its presence.

The first artificial eels and strips of mackerel that went down were instantly grabbed by outsize pollack and ling. In a mere five hours, eight men brought up 1,800 lb of predatory fish.

Rodbenders! A ling is heaved up to the surface as a big conger dives for cover.

During subsequent visits to the wreck by dedicated charter groups, ling and cod up to 40lb, pollack and coalfish of record challenging size and enormous conger were caught.

The skipper of Artilleryman II had managed to keep secret the vital Decca co-ordinate numbers of the wreck and until the inevitable day when it was discovered by the electronics of a big commercial trawler it would continue to be an anglers' paradise.

The hulk, which was estimated to be over 400 ft long, lay in the middle regions of the English Channel in the separation zone, a super highway for ships of all kinds from sizeable tramps to behmoths a thousand feet long weighing half-a-million tons.

In such company a 38ft charter boat in a waste of sea is nothing more than a piece of flotsam.

Sheer distance from land and the ever changing weather patterns of open water keeps separation zone wrecks exclusive to the most dedicated of saltwater anglers.

Participants in 'over the horizon' angling must be able to withstand hours on a heaving deck, a cold wind, perhaps driving rain, and seasickness. Otherwise such a trip can be pure hell.

For those impervious to the rigours the reward is the finest fishing in the world.

Since offshore fishing began in the middle sixties the range of operations has increased in a manner few of the pioneers would have thought possible.

Twenty miles from the coast has progressed to unlimited distance. Today, some top flight charter boat skippers who have invested heavily in craft and electronics range the whole width of the English Channel, and it takes almost a gale to halt expeditions to far off marks.

Five day charters between ports on the South Devon coast and Guernsey in the Channel Islands have become very popular with the new breed of deep sea angler.

It involves a four hour run or more, to a chosen wreck, perhaps 20 hours of actual fishing, which means right through the dark hours in dangerous waters and then a three hour run to Guernsey.

After a night on the town it's a

Artilleryman 11, Britain's fastest charter boat heads back to Plymouth at 20 knots.

Big cod and coalies on display after a successful mid-channel wrecking trip.

dawn departure from St. Peter Port for a repeat performance finally docking at Plymouth, Dartmouth, or Brixham late in the evening on the fifth day, with 3,000 lb of fish and perhaps a record-breaker in the hold.

Some groups elect to spend a second night in Guernsey and fish at wrecks lying close to the Channel Island coast before starting the long haul back to Devon stopping at wrecks on the way.

Offshore wreck fishing of this quality doesn't come cheap. The actual cost of a full day is dependent on how far from port the boat travels, time at sea being governed by distance.

The average for an individual place is about £20. But usually the long range trip is organised by a club or group who share the full coast of the boat, up to £250 per day for the extended trips.

Some prefer to have no more than half-a-dozen in the party, which guarantees a lot more room, but at a much higher individual cost. It is not unknown for just four men to charter for a five-day trip.

You can take away the entire catch but generally there are so many fish it would be totally impractical. At this high level of fishing just half a dozen ling can be turned into 50 lb of prime fillets.

A 40lb plus conger is hauled over the gunwale of Salt-wind II.

Dave Brown of Plymouth, found the British record coalfish of 37lb 5 oz swimming high over a mid-channel wreck. He was fishing a five day Channel Island charter aboard Artilleryman II.

The very hard world that is offshore wreck fishing has brought a wealth of change to the British Record list. In the early years of the sport many records which had stood for a very long time were shattered, with weights soaring to previously unthought of heights.

Conger, coalfish, pollack and cod are just a few of the species under constant attack. During the last two years the records for pollack and coalfish have changed hands four times.

Before wreck fishing it was normal for the standards of these species to remain unchallenged for 30 years and more.

The ling record of 45lb set in 1912 stood for 63 years, but since 1975 it has had four owners.

Now, the chase is on to find a pollack bigger than 27lb 6oz, a coalfish that will take a scale needle past 37lb 5oz, a conger heavier than 109lb 6oz and a ling over 57½lb.

As big as these records are, in time all will be shattered as fishing at mid-channel wrecks undergoes further expansion. Larger, much faster boats with better facilities are expected to come onto the scene before the end of this decade.

The wreck beneath our keel was obviously loaded with fish. Despite poor weather conditions ling and conger were arriving at the gunwale and being unceremoniously hauled aboard.

Several cod in the 30lb class and a dozen heavy pollack were in the fish-box which could hold 2,000 lb – it was already two-thirds full although we had been fishing only four hours.

If the boat should move off the centre-line of the wreck as the tide altered there was a good chance that a large turbot hiding in the sand at the side of the hull, would take one of the mackerel baits. Three British Records were set when this situation occurred.

The scheduled stay over the hulk was six hours and only if the wind grew stronger would a move for port begin. Even then four long unpleasant hours would pass before the boat slipped by a welcoming breakwater.

Rough water is often the companion of the offshore angler, but those who brave it to reach the many wrecks which lie far from land reckon the spoils are well worth the discomfort.

DIVISION ONE

Celebrating in style. The champagne flowed all night for Division One champions Izaak Walton (Staffs).

This 8lb 7 oz net was worth £2,500 for individual winner Mark Stabler

IZAAK WALTON (Staffs) hoisted the premier title in match angling — the NFA's Division One National Championships — with a near record points score of 815.

The 1986 event was fished on the Oxford Canal — a venue they regarded as home and it showed as they left the rest of the field standing with a 69 point winning margin.

Having practised since the start of the season they got the team plan dead right fishing bloodworm on tiny hooks and feeding with jokers to catch midget gudgeon.

Canal teams also took the next two places. Local squad Hinckley were second followed by St Helens.

The new individual champion not only had one of the lowest weights to win a National but he also only just made it on the day after his car broke down on the way.

Provincial AA's Mark Stabler netted 8lb 7oz to scoop £2,500 in prize money — enough to buy a new car for the journey home to Norton Canis, Cannock.

The design engineer spent the opening 90 minutes scratching for tiny gudgeon on the nearside shelf of his peg at Twyford until he spotted chub on the far side in nine inches of water.

A waggler fished double caster bait on an 18 hook was immediately snapped up by a 1lb chub that gave some hairy moments on a 1½lb bottom.

Sitting it out for the rest of the match he had just three more bites — two chub were landed and then in the last ten minutes a title clinching 4½lb carp.

DIVISION TWO

THE 1986 Division Two National on the Trent turned into a two horse race as Hull and Bawtry battled it out for the team honours.

Hull, relegated last year, bounced back with a Championship clinching 813 points. They had three of the top five individuals — and collected £6,000 in winnings.

Bawtry lived up to their name of the waspgrub brigade taking the individual title, two more in the top twelve and second in the team result with 708 points.

Mike Jordan, Hull manager and second individual, said: 'We got what we deserved last year but this time we developed a team plan, took it seriously and were determined to win.'

The plan of fishing the stick float with maggots worked like a dream as every team member finished in the top 25 of his section.

With four wasp nests for every angler in a chubby area, Bawtry, the 1982 Division Three champions, were well prepared while the rest of the team used maggot and caster.

A very happy and considerably richer Hull team after winning the Division Two title.

John Howard used most of his grubs to thrash the rest of the field with 41lb 14oz of chub from Caythorpe.

The Doncaster excavator driver had a pre-match premonition that he would do well and it came true with a stream of chub to 2lb.

He alternated wasp grub and caster on a feeder rig for the first two hours taking a dozen fish before switching to a waggler to catch more before two boats scattered the shoal.

A long way behind was Mick Jordan with a 19lb 6oz catch taken on single maggot and feeder from the famous aquarium swims at Holme Marsh.

Consolation for the Bawtry team in the form of individual winner John Howard with this 40 lb plus catch of chub.

N.F.A. DIVISIONAL CHAMPIONSHIPS

Date	Venue	Teams	Winners	Team weight lb	oz	dr		Individual	Individual highest weight lb	oz	dr
1906	R. Thames, Pangbourne	7	Boston	17	8	4		F. Beales (Boston)	4	11	0
1907	R. Witham, Kirkstead	13	Sheffield Amal.	21	12	12		A. Croft (Sheffield)	7	1	8
1908	North Level Drain, Tydd	13	Sheffield & Dist	18	6	0		J. Mason (Sheffield)	12	2	0
1909	The Dyke, Newark	18	Leeds Amal.	7	5	4		J.H.R. Bazley (Leeds)	2	2	8
1910	R. Derwent, Hutton's Ambo	17	Leeds Amal.	5	8	12		A. Blackman (Hull)	2	13	8
1911	R. Severn, Kimpsey	19	Sheffield Amal.	53	6	0		W. Lowe (Sheffield)	13	4	0
1912	R. Ouse, Ely	20	Boston	25	9	0		G. Beales (Boston)	6	11	12
1913	R. Dee, Chester	22	Nottingham	2	15	0		W. Gough (Nottingham)	1	14	8
1914	R. Trent, Willington	20	Leeds Amal.	20	14	8		A. Skerratt (Derby)	6	15	12
1919	R. Ancholme, Brigg	24	Boston	20	0	8		T. Hill (Derby)	7	7	0
1920	R. Weaver, Hartford	29	County Palatine	12	4	4		R. Barlow (Hull)	3	1	0
1921	R. Trent, Burton Joyce	32	Derby	10	1	0		J. Wakesfield (Derby)	6	2	12
1922	R. Witham, Kirstead	38	Lincoln	10	5	12		B. Hobday (Lincoln)	3	5	8
1923	R. Soar, Kegworth	41	County Palatine	18	11	0		J.W. Couldwell (Sheffield)	5	15	8
1924	R. Glen, Pinchbeck, Linc	43	Castleford & Dist.	28	0	8		W.T. Willcocks (London)	21	8	8
1925	R. Severn, Worcester	46	Long Eaton	5	10	8		G. Allen (Provincial)	3	8	12
1926	R. Ouse, Naburn, Yorks.	47	Lincoln	23	11	9		A. Fletcher (Boston)	7	1	0
1927	Middle Level Drain, King's Lynn, Norfolk	47	Grimsby & Dist.	44	5	12		J.H.R. Bazley (Leeds)	16	5	8
1928	R. Severn, Tewkesbury	44	Leeds & Dist.	13	2	13		W. Tetley (Leeds)	3	13	3
1929	R. Witham Kirkstead	44	Boston	50	4	0		J. Sykes (Boston)	10	15	0
1930	R. Soar, Kegworth, Derby	51	Sheffield Amal.	43	10	0		C. Muddimer (Leicester)	15	6	0
1931	South Forty Foot Drain	48	Hull Amal.	27	9	8		O. Daddy (HUll)	19	9	8
1932	R. Soar, Kegworth, Derby	47	Loughborough	24	15	0		H. Sallis (Long Eaton)	5	9	4
1933	R. Great Ouse, Olney, Bucks	48	Sheffield & Dist.	33	6	4		Edgar Dabill (Sheffield)	13	15	9
1934	R. Thames, Abingdon, Berks	54	Sheffield Amal.	14	3	11		H. Smith (Sheffield)	4	14	4
1935	R. Witham, Kirkstead, Lincs.	50	Lincoln	43	13	2		A. Kellett (Doncaster)	18	6	15
1936	R. Thurne, Potter Heigham	53	Lincoln	74	5	15		A.E. Bryant (Buckingham)	35	1	0
1937	Gloucester Canal	56	Groves & Whitnall	23	15	6		H. Jones (Co. Palatine)	9	9	9
1938	R. Great Ouse, Harrold	62	Hull & Dist.	38	12	7		G. Bright (Bristol)	21	13	8
1945	R. Trent, Newark, Notts	57	Worksop	75	2	5		M.T. Cotteril (Worksop)	16	1	7
1945	R. Trent, Newark, Notts.	57	Worksop	75	2	5		M.T. Cotteril (Worksop)	16	1	7
1946	R. Witham, Langrick, Notts	66	Hull	57	0	12		G. Laybourne (York)	12	12	8
1947	R. Witham, Kirkstead, Lincs.	70	Worksop	57	8	4		W. Edwards (Rotherham)	9	4	8
1948	R. Huntspill, Somerset	72	Leeds Amal.	23	14	4		W. Thompson (Leeds)	14	9	12
1949	R. Thurne, Potter Heigham	77	Leeds Amal.	49	3	4		R. Woodhall (Whit. Reans)	15	6	8
1950	R. Nene, Peterborough	81	Peterborough	62	5	12		W. Rockley (Peterborough)	15	4	0
1951	R. Witham, Kirkstead, Lincs	82	Doncaster	93	5	0		S. Buxton (Doncaster)	20	13	4
1952	R. Severn, Bridgnorth, Salop	88	Leeds Amal.	135	5	0		H. Seed (Leeds)	33	5	4
1953	R. Nene, Peterborough	92	Lincoln	72	5	0		N. Hazelwood (Cmb.)	27	14	0
1954	R. Trent, Gunthorpe, Notts	98	Hull Angling Pres.	68	13	1		R. Lye (Notts. Fed.)	15	1	12
1955	R. Huntspill, Somerset	99	Sheffield Amal.	136	15	4		J. Carr (Sheffield Amal.)	68	2	4
1956	R. Witham, Kirkstead, Lincs	94	Coventry & Dist.	86	4	4		C.R. Lusby (Lincoln)	25	8	0
1957	R. Severn, Bridgnorth, Salop	96	Notts. A.A.	22	8	1		H. Story (Notts. A.A.)	7	12	8
1958	R. Welland, Spalding, Lincs.	98	Coventry A.A.	59	15	4		W. Hughes (Northern A.A.)	24	3	0
1959	R Nene, Peterborough	100	Bedford A.C.	86	1	4		J. Sharpe (Bedford)	57	8	8
1960	Rs. Ante, Bure, Thurne, Nflk.	101	King's Lynn A.A.	81	15	1		K. Smith (Norwich)	50	14	8
1961	R. Trent, Nottingham	103	Coventry A.A.	77	6	12		J. Blakey (Saltaire)	23	12	12
1962	R. Welland, Spalding Lincs.	103	Lincoln	56	2	12		V.A. Baker (Derby Railway)	13	11	0
1963	Gloucester Canal	105	Northampton Nene A.C.	19	11	2		R. Sims (N. Som. & West Wilts.)	14	15	2
1964	R. Severn, Worcester	107	Kidderminster	50	13	2		G. Burch (Essex County)	32	3	0
1965	R. Huntspill, Somerset	110	Rugby Federation	93	7	8		D. Burr (Rugby)	76	9	0
1966	R. Witham, Lincs	108	Boston	75	1	4		R. Jarvis (Boston)	29	1	8
1967	Relief Channel, Norfolk	111	Derby Railway	83	4	4		E. Townsin (Cambridge F.P.)	40	6	8
1968	Rs. Ante, Bure, Thurne, Nflk.	112	Leighton Buzzard	74	0	8		D. Groom (Leighton Buzzard)	36	6	0
1969	R. Trent, Nottingham	114	Stoke	32	8	2		R. Else (Lincoln)	9	7	3
1970	Middle Level Drain	113	Cambridge F.P.S.	97	2	0		B. Lakey (Cambridge)	35	4	8
1971	R. Severn, Stourport	116	Leicester	124	8	8		R. Harris (Peterborough)	40	5	0
1972	Div.1: Bristol Avon	79	Birmingham A.A.	51	1	12	248	P. Coles (Leicester)	33	8	0
	Div.2: R Welland	81	Coleshill, Warks.	72	15	8	216	J. Hart	54	14	8

N.F.A. DIVISIONAL CHAMPIONSHIPS

CONTINUED FROM PREVIOUS PAGE

Date	Venue	Teams	Winners	Team weight lb	oz	dr	Team points		Individual highest weight lb	oz	dr
1973	Div.1: R. Witham	80	Grimsby A.S.A.	92	10	4	717	A. Wright (Derby Rly Inst.)	41	10	8
	Div.2: Gt Ouse Relief Channel	92	Leigh & Dist. (Lancs.)	76	6	8	826	J. Wilkinson (Elthorne A.S., Hanwell)	43	1	8
1974	Div.1: R. Welland	80	Leicester A.S.	25	9	4	733	P. Anderson (Cambridge F.P.A.S.)	40	2	8
	Div.2: Avon (Warks.)	85	Stockport Fed.	71	0	8	1161	C. Hibbs (Leigh Miners)	47	3	8
1975	Div.1: R. Nene	79	Birmingham A.A.	43	15	12	814	M. Hoad-Reddick (Rotherham U.A.F.)	63	7	0
	Div.2. R. Trent	71	Long Eaton Victoria A.S., Nottingham	60	6	4	735	A. Webber (Wigan)	16	2	8
	Div.3: R. Welland	42	Crawley A.S., Sussex	18	9	0	394	J. Garrett (GEC Marconi, Chelmsford)	24	8	0
1976	Div.1: R. Trent	79	Birmingham A.A.	53	14	4	776	N. Wells (Newark)	28	0	8
	Div.2: R. Witham	76	Izaak Walton (Preston) A.S.	34	14	8	783	P. Marks (Exeter)	12	11	8
	Div.3: R. Huntspill South and King's Sedgemoor Drains	80	London A.A.	47	6	4	693	D. Knox (Cheadle)	39	9	12
1977	Div.1: R. Welland	77	Coventry A.A.	25	15	4	755	R. Foster (Rotherham)	39	10	4
	Div.2: Gt. Ouse	72	Huntingdon A.S.	34	10	12	687	S. Yeomans (Reading)	24	3	0
	Div.3: R. Trent	90	Stratford upon Avon	30	9	0	881	C. Robinson (Barnet)	18	4	8
1978	Div.1: Bristol Avon	79	Coleshill & Dist. A.S.	84	11	8	790	D. Harris (Bradford City)	48	13	0
	Div.2: R. Trent	78	Nottingham A.A.	36	13	4	806	I. Carrier (Long Eaton)	10	5	8
	Div.3: R. Witham	74	Bathampton A.A.	33	13	4	712	L. Constable (Chatteris)	29	8	8
	Div.4: R. Huntspill South & King's Sedgemoor Drains	34	Swindon Talisman A.C.	30	1	0	353	B. Shepherd (Ramsey & Dist. A.C.)	56	2	0
1979	Div.1: Gt. Ouse and R. Cam	80	Barnsley	10	15	4	700	M. Cullen (Oxford & Dist.)	11	8	0
	Div.2: R. Witham	80	Bathampton A.A.	32	2	0	746	S. White (Leek & Morelands)	11	13	0
	Div.3: R. Welland and Coronation Channel	73	Swindon Talisman A.C.	56	1	8	769	P. Deacon (Welling & Dist.)	17	5	0
	Div.4: R. Trent	56	Marazion A.C.	79	12	8	571	G. Salisbury (Marazion A.C.)	34	6	0
1980	Div.1: R. Trent	80	Nottingham Fed.	93	5	12	883	P. Burrell (Essex County)	27	8	0
	Div.2: R. Witham	74	Oundle	33	10	8	735	D. Green (Boston)	46	0	0
	Div.3: R. Ancholme	68	Wisbech	42	1	0	664	A. Kelly (Kidsgrove)	13	1	8
	Div.4: Yorks, Ouse	52	Telford (Salop)	7	13	12	461	D. Hall (Stoke)	6	10	8
1981	Div.1: R. Ancholme	79	Essex County	19	7	0	714	D. Steer (CALPAC)	21	3	0
	Div.2: Leeds Liverpool Canal	73	Southport D.A.A.	52	3	4	687	D. Sayce (Luton)	16	15	0
	Div.3: Oxford Canal	71	North Staffs.	25	15	8	741	B. Clampitt (L'head)	18	10	8
	Div.4: R. Thames	80	Lamb A.C.	53	4		764	P. Hamlyn (Maidstone)	20	0	8
1982	Div.1: R. Huntspill South & King's Sedgemoor Drains	78	Rotherham	27	0	4	718	Alan Mayer (Stockport Fed.)	21	13	0
	Div.3: R. Trent	76	Bawtry A.C.	64	4	0	741	R. Moir (Hayes & Harlington A.S.)	27	15	8
	Div.4: Leeds Liverpool Canal	78	Congleton A.C.	36	12	0	741	E. Townsin (Ely Sugar)	8	13	0
1983	Div.1: R. Trent	79	Nottingham Fed.	141	1	0	741	D. Howl (Atherstone)	42	9	6
	Div.2: Yorkshire Ouse	74	Redditch & Dist.	39	1	4	689	A. Whitehead (Winsford)	12	15	10
	Div.3: Oxford Canal	73	Northern A.A. (Blackburn Centre)	27	10	3	724	W. Pearce (Lamb A.C.)	9	10	1
	Div.4: R. Witham	89	Kirkstead A.C.	44	8	1	980	A. Curd (Rye & Dist.)	22	3	13
1984	Div.1: R. Nene	77	Coleshill and Dist. A.A.	39	1	4	672	C. Gregg (Worcester)	42	11	2
	Div.2: Grand Union Canal	78	Southport D.A.A.	42	2	0	873	C. Hibbs (Leigh and Dist.)	10	1	2
	Div.3: R. Trent	73	Catch Match	65	8	9	680	M. Day (Travellers)	43	7	13
	Div.4: R. Ancholme	96	Weybridge	16	13	4	990	R. Ayre (Pendle)	34	11	1
1985	Div.1: Leeds-Liverpool Canal	79	ABC	20	13	0	712	B. Oliver (Northwich)	9	6	4
	Div.2: R.Witham	79	Kirkstead	35	3	0	734	M. Hukin (Darnall)	13	14	0
	Div.3: R. Thames	78	Letchworth D.A.A.	84	2	0	833	M. O'Neill (Manchester)	60	6	0
	Div.4: R. Trent	75	Cove A.S.	58	13	0	691	I. Bristow (Derby)	32	5	0
	Div.5: R. Trent	43	Trevs A.S.	71	5	0	372	D. Weston (Royal Oak)	49	14	0
1986	Div.1 Oxford Canal	78	Izaak Walton (Staffs)	29	12	12	815	Mark Stabler (Provincial A.A.)	8	7	0
	Div.2: R. Trent	76	Hull	99	3	8	813	J. Howard (Bawtry)	41	14	0
	Div.3: Royal Military Canal	74	Starlets	60	14	13		P. Barber (Reddish A.C.)	75	9	0
	Div.4: R. Witham	75	Trevs	46	7	2	779	P. Stanton (Wadsley Bridge)	17	3	0
	Div.5: Lancaster Canal	57	Lansil A.C.	34	11	8	589	A. Holdsworth (Pendle and Burnley A.A.)	11	14	8

DIVISION THREE

A triumphant Starlets squad captained for 16 years by former England international Mark Downes in the middle

One more bream would have given Peter Barber the record but with 75lb 9 oz he was still a clear winner.

STOCKPORT matchman Pete Barber walked the Division Three event on the Royal Military Canal with the second heaviest weight ever taken in a National Championships.

Within 15 minutes of the whistle, the Reddish AC team man was into the first of 29 bream for a stunning weight of 75lb 9oz — just 1lb off the record weight.

Fish to 3½ lb kept coming to waggler fished single caster, doubles and cocktails with worm on hook sizes ranging from 22 to a 16.

The water in front of him was thick with bream and any mistake would have scattered the shoal. Each fish was played very carefully. He only lost five of which two were thought to be tench, and the shoal was kept occupied by loose feeding casters.

A purposely undershotted float fished a foot over-depth prevented him from striking at false bites and after a couple of pre-match bets he took home £3,000.

Red-hot favourites Starlets turned in a brilliant performance to win the team match with 742 points, only 49 ahead of Weybridge.

Intensive practise sessions fine-tuned the Starlets approach of fishing half size gozzers near the bottom on the pole and small waggler.

They fished light, 22 hooks to 12 ounce bottoms, and fed sloppy groundbait to build up a mid-canal catching area that put seven of their men in the top ten of their section.

Weybridge were pleased with their performance as they consider themselves specialist canal anglers.

DIVISION FOUR

HOT favourites Trev's Compalite lifted their second National trophy in two years when they won the 1986 Division Four match on the Witham.

Fresh from their Division Five triumph on the Trent, the slick London outfit didn't take it easy and worked hard for their 779 points triumph.

A Close Season walkabout was followed by a month's practise and a peg by peg breakdown formulated with Rotherham ace Jack Pugh. The team plan worked perfectly.

Champions twice in two years — that's Trevs pictured here after their 1986 victory on the Witham.

Despite blustery wind every man fished like a professional with an 11 metre pole to finish well up in their sections after catching on a waggler rig with bloodworm or squatts.

Gloucester team Gordon League earned a place on the River Severn for the next year's Division Three match by finishing second with 708 points.

A painful attack of shingles nearly prevented individual champion Paul Stanton from fishing the match.

After a couple of painkillers he decided to go ahead and when he got to his peg on the Whitehouse Bend the Wadsley Bridge angler knew he had made the right choice as it was a noted bream spot.

Ignoring the team plan of going for eels he opted for feeder fished gozzers, red maggots or bloodworm to take 17lb 3oz of bream.

Paul included fish to 3lb in his catch which also earned him a few bob after betting £5 at 500-1 odds.

Eddie Townsin of Ely Beet Sports came close to winning his third National when he finished second with 15lb 14oz of bream from a peg at Stixwould.

The pain goes when you're a winner as Paul Stanton found out after becoming champion with his big bream catch.

DIVISION FIVE

Clear winners Lansil AC after their Division Five victory.

Alan Holdsworth made a clean sweep of the individual stakes with nearly 12 lb of small fish.

LOCAL favourites Lansil AC came home as clear winners in the Division Five National — beating 56 other teams and the bookmakers.

Knowledge of the Lancaster Canal and a crack squad boosted by three England men scored 589 points.

Sticking to team tactics of bloodworm fed across for bream while catching small fish on the inside at the start also earned them a few bob — each team member had a £20 bet at pre-match odds of 30-1.

The squad was skippered by non-fishing captain Graham Joynt — the first man to introduce the pole and bloodworm to the Lancaster Canal.

Only other team with a chance was Glevum which was made up of the Shakespeare anglers who fished like professionals to take second with 533 points.

Shining through as individual champion was Alan Holdsworth of Pendle and Burnley AA who netted 11lb 14½oz of small fish.

The chimney sweep started by emptying, at the 13 metre mark, three quarters of a pint of bloodworm — bait that he had scraped on the eve of the match for himself and his team-mates.

His first hour was spent scratching for roach but by then the skimmers had moved over his baited area.

Changing to a gozzer/bloodworm cocktail on an 18 hook he pushed the pole out to its full length and never looked back taking fish to 8oz every cast.

With two hours to go a boat ploughed through his swim. Another half pint of bloodworm bought it back to life giving Alan a memorable and well deserved win.

Pat Needham had her prayers answered with this 10 lb ¾ oz winning catch in the Ladies National.

LADIES NATIONAL CHAMPIONSHIPS

SHEFFIELD housewife Pat Needham ignored the advice of her husband Brian and went on to win the title that has eluded her for so long — the NFA Ladies National.

Having twice claimed second and third place in the event Pat (Oakley's Tackle) had her pre-match prayers answered after landing 10lb ¾oz of chub from the Island swim on the Warwickshire Avon at Twyford Farm.

The peg was a noted bream spot and Brian told her to fish down the inside with caster. He then went down the pub!

But Pat spotted a shoal of chub on the surface and by trotting a light stickfloat down the middle landed 30 on caster.

Only one fish short of the Championship was Portsmouth grandmother Edna White who took 14 chub to 1lb on a swimfeeder rig and double caster for 9lb 13oz.

First cast for Rene Horne (Basingstoke) produced a 1½ lb chub but the twice former winner had to work hard for the rest of her third placed 8lb 1oz net as a stream of boats ploughed through her peg.

NATIONAL JUNIOR CHAMPIONSHIP

Junior Champion and his catch... Richard Stimpson with his 12 lb plus bream net that gave him the individual title.

MILTON KEYNES AA really slayed the opposition in their first Junior National on the Grand Union Canal!

With two section winners and every team member finishing in the top 20 of their section they amassed 594 points, in the 1986 Championships — 22 ahead of their nearest rivals.

Team tactics to fish the nearside with squatts on the pole combined with a local knowledge of the canal from Wolverhampton to Leighton Buzzard beat 54 other teams.

A good all-round performance with three anglers in the top 11 gave Mansfield AA second spot with 572 points from a venue they had never seen before.

Ever consistent Leicester juniors were third with 534 points. Despite having won the event three times they were not disappointed as they do not consider themselves canal anglers.

Bream basher Richard Stimpson was a convincing individual winner after he landed seven fish for 12lb 6oz 12dr.

Starting on team tactics of waggler down the middle, with squatts, the Oxford DAA angler took five perch before he heard of his peg's potential.

A hole in the far side was a noted bream spot and a quick change to link legered maggots on his dad's quivertip rod bought immediate success.

He took five bream in quick succession before two boats ploughed through his swim leaving him only two more bream in the final hour.

Richard not only won the Championship but also a bet with his dad John for £1 per lb of fish caught.

Jubilant Milton Keynes AA, winners of a Junior National at their first attempt.

Date	Venue	Teams	Winners	Team weight lb	oz	dr	Team Points		Individual highest weight lb	oz	dr
1978	Leeds-Liverpool Canal	56	Stockport & Dist.	21	1	4	611	A. Hunt (Coventry)	8	4	0
1979	Warwickshire Avon	51	Bristol and West	33	2	8	491	G. Bennett (B'ham)	17	10	0
1980	R. Trent	70	Leicester A.S.	27	2	12	708	P. Matthews (Newark)	16	10	0
1981	Leeds-Liverpool Canal	60	Northern A.A.	13	0	0	655	M. Church (Long Eaton Vic.)	5	8	4
1982	R. Thames	60	Peterborough	48	15	11	647	D. Rose (Stratford-on-Avon)	13	5	0
1983	Suffolk Stour	46	Leicester A.A.	19	0	5	473	G. Robinson (Oxford DAA)	12	7	14
1984	Lancaster Canal	58	St. Helens A.A.	15	10	0	687	S. McKenna (Northern A.A.)	4	8	15
1985	R. Trent	59	Leicester A.S.	46	8	0	602	C. Chesters (Leicester)	20	2	0
1986	Grand Union Canal	55	Milton Keynes A.A.	22	4	8	594	R. Stimpson (Oxford D.A.A.)	12	6	12

The magic of A

MOST of us have a favourite fishing place where we feel completely at ease and certain of enjoying ourselves.

In Britain there are just two waters which have that special attraction for me.

For Scottish holidays there is the remote Loch Urigill in Sutherland where the wild brown trout fishing is fabulous, the fishing conditions varied and the surroundings majestic. You rarely see another boat on the wide expanse of peaty water.

Close to home are the contrasting charms of Avington Trout Lakes with their parkland setting, crystal clear water from the Itchen and large stocked rainbows which are rarely as easy to catch as people imagine.

To complete the contrast you can on some days get a rush of anglers for the nine o'clock start and some jockeying for favoured positions.

That is a combination which suits well; the distant well-remembered water visited once a year and providing total change to the pleasures of the local familiar Hampshire fishery.

To complete the enjoyment there has to be the stimulus of trying also new waters, new methods. But for me Avington is the special attraction, returned to so often because it is touched with magic.

The essence of magic, of course, is its capacity to surprise you and the fact that not everyone can see how the trick is worked.

The surprises at Avington can be in the size of fish caught in a water which has yielded the UK record in rainbows and in brook trout, and always has some heavy fish to be hunted. There's also the different moods of the trout and the way the hotspots may change from day to day.

The failure to see how the trick is worked means that not everyone catches well at Avington and not everyone appreciates its deceptively casual air.

Some come expecting there will be large trout crawling up the bank to greet them, and are surprised at how hard it can be to catch well on simple-looking lakes.

Some won't adapt method to the ways that work best at Avington. Some are put off because every fish they catch is not logged for posterity with a probably fictional entry about the fly on which it was caught.

How spurious some of those can be was nicely illustrated for me in a big fish lake where the records showed famous big trout hunter Alan Pearson catching four monsters on corixa.

'Don't often see you fishing with corixa,' I said to him, having observed that the next 20 fish were also entered as caught on corixa.

'It was a large Jack Frost in fact, but why shouldn't they work it out for themselves like I had to,' was Alan's response.

So were the other 20 kidding too - or did everyone thereafter fish with corixa, following Alan's entry so that nothing else was on offer? The only certain lesson was not to put much reliance on book entries, which is why Avington has none.

Part of the attraction for me then is in the informality. Fishing can only be enjoyed to the full when it is a relaxed pastime and Avington is singularly free of regimentation and mass of regulations, with which some others clutter themselves.

A single fly not more than one inch in overall length, a limit of four fish from lakes and two from stream, all fish caught to be killed, none under a pound to count are the simple basic rules.

That apart the place is kept tidy the lakes well-stocked and it is up to you to sort how to catch the sometimes perverse fish. Just the place for a happy-go-lucky angler like myself; and at Avington I am indeed always happy, often lucky.

Delight in angling depends on many things, but for most people the fishing and the setting predominate. If these are right the rest follows as naturally as the love of a sport inborn in millions of us.

So what is special about the Avington fishing? Well, for a start there are the fish. You don't get many under two pounds and the average size is around 2½lb.

Fishing on average once a week, and usually turning up on odd days without pre-booking, all the fish I have caught have been in excellent condition.

Avington is open all year for rainbow trout and on the few occasions I have sampled the winter fishing the trout were remarkably plump and silvery.

Then there is always the hope of a big fish, and the knowledge that there are at least one or two there somewhere. My own preference is that the large one comes as a pleasant surprise rather than setting out to stalk them as experts

Tony Pawson and vividly marked rainbow from Avington that protested all the way to the net.

vington

By Tony Pawson

A day-ticket at Avington includes the right to hook a brace from this Itchen tributary which loops through the fishery.

like Surrey's Peter Cockwill do.

Even so I have had my share of trout between six and eight pounds. Indeed one of my more entertaining moments was to take some of them from the deep freeze to be smoked, and have to wait while a group ahead of me were chatting about the decline in standards of trout at Avington.

Happily they asked where my fish came from as I emptied the sacks - then changed the subject abruptly.

Avington held the rainbow record for many years and sooner or later it's possible a 25-pounder will come from there - indeed may already have done so after this piece was written. For there have been rumours of a fish in this class being released and evading anglers.

Only a season ago there was a hump-backed fish I saw that must have been 20lb, but so far I know Quasimodo, as we christened him, was never hooked.

That is another interesting aspect of the Avington trout. There are usually a few recently stocked fish, which are relatively easy to catch early on if you fish sensibly for them. But it does not even take them an hour to become fully acclimatised once the artificials thud in around them.

There was a good example of this when a practice was fished at Avington to test it out as a venue for the final part of the individual event in the World Championships.

The selected England team fished a friendly match against a Lords and Commons team, and an international team. In the first half-hour period John Golding caught three in an area where there were several stock fish.

Thereafter others equally knowledgable about Avington found it hard to catch even one there, though there were still plenty of fish circling that spot.

Either they had learnt quick or John, a formidable competitor, had thrown a brick in before leaving.

No need for any such suspicion as the manager, Roy Ward, who knows his trout better than anyone else, confirms often to me that this quick adaptation from easy to catch to hard to deceive is a characteristic of Avington fish.

Indeed that day the fishing followed a normal Avington pattern — some easy fish in the first hour, more difficult fishing thereafter, but the trout coming on the move again at intervals, particularly when any part had been rested for a time.

The large ones were also slower

to show than the smaller variety, with two seven-pounders caught in mid-afternoon. Those who had learnt the tricks of getting their flies down to where the fish were, of spotting fish, of how to achieve the induced takes as alternative to the standard retrieve, all did better than those who used the straightforward tactics of other stillwaters.

Fish and fishing are both interesting at Avington and it does need some learning how to fish it well - which is probably why it is not too popular with those who can't take the trouble, or expect too much in the way of weight and numbers.

On my own experience you always have a good chance of a limit in the lakes and an occasional chance of a really big fish IF you fish it well.

A digression here on 'limititis' about which weird views are often promulgated. Only fishermen could pretend that it is more interesting to be fishing in a way calculated not to catch fish, than trying to be skilful enough to hook the trout.

No reason therefore why any angler should not aim at catching the relatively low limits set - particularly as all fishing managers will ensure that not may of us can consistently achieve even that, thereby driving prices up too high or bankrupting them!

The only aspect in which the 'limititis' urge is unfortunate is if the catching of a limit becomes for you the touchstone of a good or bad day. If you can't enjoy your fishing UNLESS you catch a limit, then it is unfortunate, but only for yourself as you will destroy the pleasure of much of your fishing.

The other attraction of Avington for me is its peaceful parkland setting and the changing beauty of the surroundings from the bright colours of spring to the darker hues of autumn.

There is as much change to be noted there as in the changing lies of the trout. On the furthest lake for instance the trout traditionally holed up in the two deep parts at either end, to such a degree that Roy excavated some more holes to spread them.

Being at one with nature is a main attraction in fishing, for we are both behaving as nature intended and enjoying the natural world. In that too Avington is rewarding with plenty of fly life, plenty of bird life, however irritating the swans may be on occasion as they cruise majestically to the spot you were about to cover.

Then there are the welcoming dogs, goats, and peacocks. The humans have a part to play too for there is usually friendly interchange at Avington.

The crafty gathering for the nine o'clock dash may seem a little ridiculous, but provides much innocent fun. The wait to go down to the lakes also provides good opportunity for chat and introductions or meeting old acquaintances.

As on every other small stillwater there are some who crowd you on occasions, some who ignore the normal courtesies, but at Avington many more whom it is a pleasure to meet.

Part of its magic for those ready to absorb its atmosphere is that it is a friendly place and that rubs off on many who fish there.

How appropriate that is for a fishery so close to the tomb of Izaak Walton, our father of fishing, who regarded all anglers as brothers. Those who appreciate that approach find it easy to be part of Avington's magic circle.

Early season on the top lake at Avington and Tony Pawson is stuck fast into a hard running rainbow.

HIS FIRST 'DOUBLE'

Pete Henwood, chairman of the Association of Barbel Enthusiasts, dreamed of catching a double-figure specimen of his favourite species — but never expected it to come from Bedfordshire's Great Ouse.

Never, that is, until he hooked this 11lb 2oz beauty from a stretch at Bletsoe that he was tackling for the first time.

Pete, a 35-year-old pensions manager from Romford, Essex expected small to medium sized barbel from a swim with a sunken willow tree but it was the huge fish which picked up his swimfeedered double maggot bait.

PICTURE: TIM SCRIVENER

IF you've never sampled the sea sport around Alderney then you've missed a real treat.

The scenery is magnificent but the quality of the fishing is even better. There are heavyweights of most species and local divers say they've seen wrasse approaching 20lb!

Sole of 2½lb are common and for mainland anglers there's the opportunity to catch mullet in the very depths of winter.

TREVOR HOUSBY describes the sport fishing found in the seas around this most northern of the Channel Islands group on page 82.

Paradise Island

The rugged Alderney coastline offers deep water fishing at close range.

A visiting angler tries his luck at sunset from the rocks in Braye Bay. It's a super mark for mullet.

Jersey angler Rob Carbalistier holds up a meaty wrasse taken on hard backed crab.

A typical wrasse mark on the south side of Alderney.

Stillwater chub are still something of a rarity so lake owner Ken Wright (left) was pleased when these specimens of 4lb 6oz and 4lb 3oz turned up at his MBK Leisure fishery at Liss in Hampshire.

Holding the smaller fish is Steve Tinsley of Bromley, Kent, who like Ken caught his chub on floatfished maggot.

PICTURE: KEVIN SMITH

It was so cold that the rivers froze over and several inches of snow covered nearby fields – but it didn't deter this young angler from enjoying an afternoon's fishing at a favourite spot on Newark's River Devon.

After a spell of ice-breaking Stephen Gray from Newark was able to clear a big enough hole in the ice and the reward for his efforts was a catch of small roach.

PICTURE: RODNEY COLDRON

Essex County's Richard Banbury nets a bream from picturesque Horsens Lake in Denmark as his side move to a comfortable victory in the first ever Tuborg Cup.

The Essex lads had more than 40 lb to spare

Up for the Cup in Denmark

over their nearest rivals, Nottingham AA, with Goole and Isfield trailing well behind in the four team final.

Richard, from Basildon, Essex, also netted County's top catch (inset) at a shade over 27lb although he had to settle for second individual place behind Nottingham's John Johnson who was just over 1lb in front of him.

PICTURES: BILL BAYLISS

Shawn Sorrenson from Hull, Humberside holds aloft a double-figure cod he caught off the local port of Bridlington.

Shawn was one of ten British Aerospace club anglers who shared a monster 2,500lb haul of cod and ling – thanks to the skill of skipper Tony Pocklington who pinpointed a little known wreck a dozen miles out and then anchored over it with super accuracy.

The ten anglers bucked the area trend of fishing with muppets and jiggers and baited up with large chunks of mackerel or fresh mussels to land fish to 20lb and set a possible port record.

PICTURE: DENNIS LINLEY

Angler's Mail Assistant Editor COLIN MITCHELL helps pick a basic pole fishing outfit

WHICH POLE?

THERE are hundreds of smart poles on the market — but the most expensive is not necessarily the best.

My advice is to purchase the longest pole you can possibly afford. Invest in a nine metre, model and you will quickly discover that all the fish live at ten metres range!

Long poles — providing they are take-apart — can always be fished at shorter lengths. Don't buy a telescopic pole unless you want a specialist tool such as a whip for fishing to hand at short range.

The pole should be rigid with no signs of sag in the middle when it is at full length. And you must be able to get your hand around the thickest section.

Choose a pole that's as slim as possible for the price you can afford. Besides being cumbersome and heavy, thicker poles catch the breeze more easily and that makes them difficult to hold.

Make sure the joints take-apart without sticking. Rub them down slightly if they stick or use some form of lubricant.

Try and obtain a spare tip. Preferably, you want a thin, hollow tip to fit an internal or external elastic — and a flick tip for use without elastic.

Finally, shop around before buying. The difference in pole prices can be staggering.

PRESENTATION IS BETTER

POLE fishing rigs are made up with the same principles in mind as when fishing a float on traditional rod and line.

The one big difference is that a pole allows you to present the terminal tackle far more precisely.

Where you may fish a string of five No. 6 shot under a stick float with a domed top you may be able to present a bristle topped float carrying the equivalent of less than half that weight with the pole.

The line from pole tip to float is direct. There's no surplus line to catch the wind or surface drift.

The advantages here are obvious. Less weight means the bait can be presented much more naturally which has got to increase catch rates. There's also less water disturbance and less weight from float and shot to be felt by fish.

Those swims underneath far side bushes on canals can only be fully exploited with a pole.

The water under the bush, virgin territory for a baited hook, can be reached with the pole.

Just a couple of inches of line is left between pole tip and float. This allows a tiny waggler or stick to be pushed under the water to surface *under* the bush where you will find the fish that more confident.

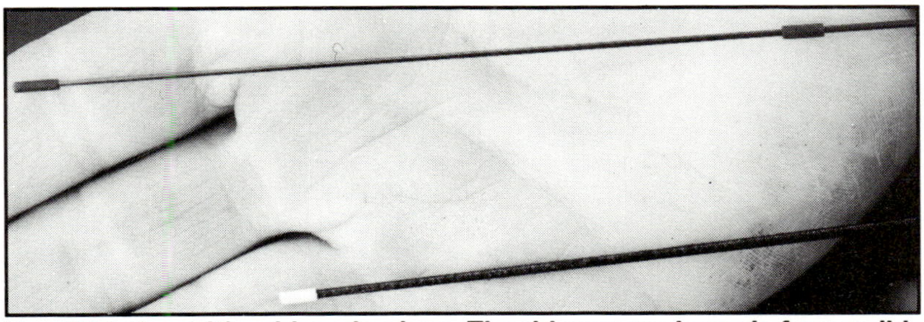

Two flick tips with rubbers in place. The thinner one is made from solid carbon fibre which makes it softer and flexible than the thicker hollow glass tip.

Flick-tip assembly

A POLE can basically be fished with two more different tip sections. Use a flick tip for small to medium-sized fish. But fit elastic to the tip when chasing bigger fish or fishing with light lines.

The flick tip is the easiest method to describe. The tip needs to be as fine as possible. Your line is fastened to it by means of silicon rubbers.

The line is threaded through two rubbers and the first one slid down the tip for about eight inches until it is a tight fit.

The second rubber is then slipped over the final tip of the pole after the line has been wrapped around the flick tip about eight or nine times.

Try and allow a bit of rubber to hang over the end of the tip as this helps prevent tangles. It may look flimsy, but it takes a mighty strong straight pull to force that line out of the rubbers.

There are many ways of fixing the elastic. It can either go through the inside of a tip or it can be fixed, via small eyes, to the outside of the tip.

The simplest way is shown in the pictures. The line is held at the bottom of the tip with a plug and at the tip end it goes through a bush which stops it being frayed.

It is stopped from going back inside the pole by using a special shop-bought toggle to which both your line and elastic are fastened.

The main thing to remember is to match the strength of your elastic to the strength of trace you are using. Elastic comes in three main strengths, light, medium and heavy.

Barbless mishaps

YOU don't require special hooks for pole fishing – but avoid barbless patterns unless you are catching small fish at close range and swinging them to hand.

Hooks with micro or whisker barbs are best for pole sport, especially when unshipping sections.

Even the most experienced anglers find that barbless hooks lose fish, both big and small, when pushing back a long pole before taking it apart so fish can either be swung to hand or netted.

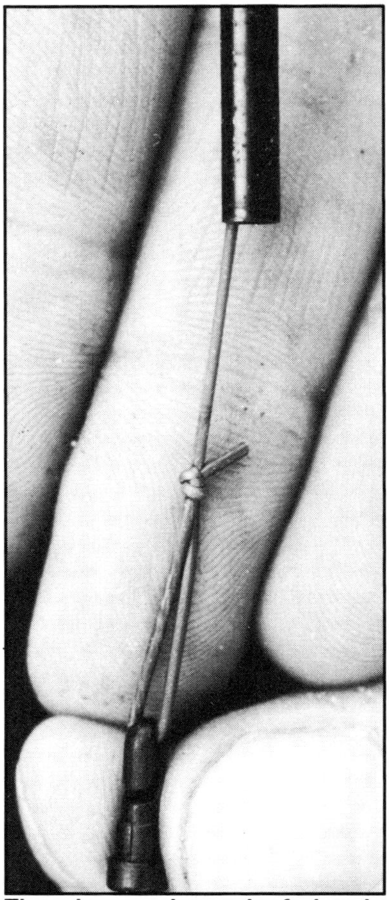

The plug at the end of the tip section which holds the internal elastic in place.

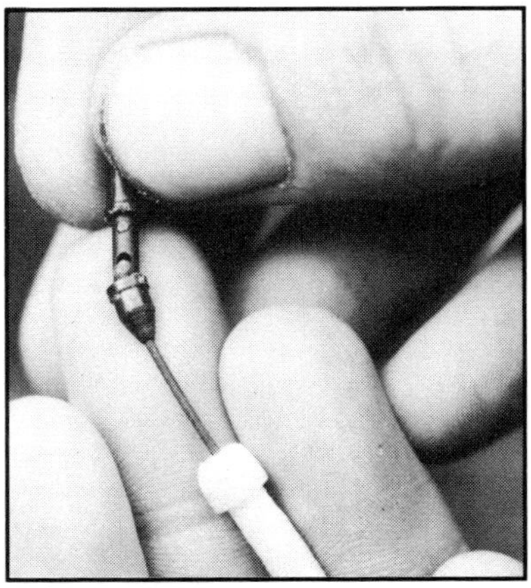

The thinner end of the pole for fishing elastic. The white bush stops the elastic from fraying. The connector holds the line and elastic.

Wire used for threading plastic through a pole tip.

These accessories make life easier

Roller to help shove the pole back smoothly and support a lengthy section.

THERE are numerous accessories for pole anglers many of which become indespensible once you have used them.

The ROLLER enables you to push back the pole when unshipping sections without scratching them on the bank. It will also support a long pole to prevent worries about breaking.

A POLE REST, in the form of a cradle for the front and an upturned U shape for the back one means fairly long poles can hold tackle out over water without the angler having to sit like a stone statue waiting for bites.

POLE HOLDERS push into the ground and the tube that is left showing holds the pole in a vertical position so that it doesn't get trod on or the line tangled in long grass.

ANCHORS are invaluable if you carry around – as you should – ready made up rigs on winders. Rigs are put onto winders hook first so that the last thing hanging off is your loop of line.

Anchors slip into this loop and then a ring on the other end of the rubber anchor hooks over the winder itself to keep the rig in place.

LASLUBE is a form of lubrication which is pushed into the end of poles so that elastic can run freely without sticking.

A DOSAPIOMBOI is a handy gadget to help you make up pole rigs at home. Pole floats clip onto this plastic item which has a neutral gravity in water.

Weights are then placed on a rim under the float clip which enables you to find out - without putting line through the float - just what its shot carrying capacity is.

WIRE is an important item for anyone fishing internal elastic. The wire helps to pull the elastic through the pole tip. Just try threading anything from three-quarters of a metre to two metres of elastic through a tip and you will see why this is true!

STYLS are tiny weights used instead of split shot on pole rigs. They weigh less than our smallest shot and their tubular shape with a split down the side for your line means that they fall much more naturally through the water with a bait.

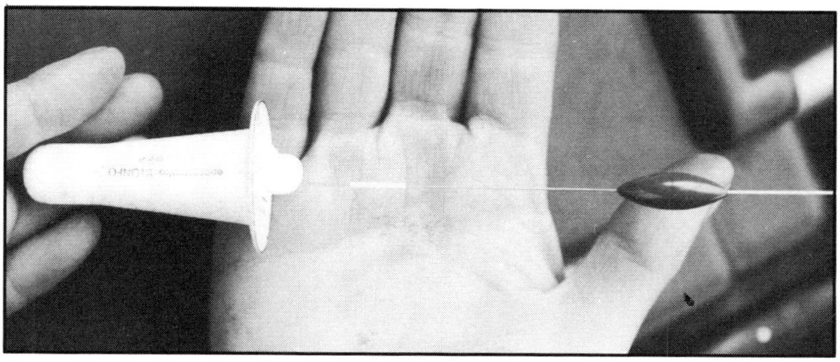

Dosapiombo for shotting up floats at home

Pole rest, cupped front and upturned U rear rest

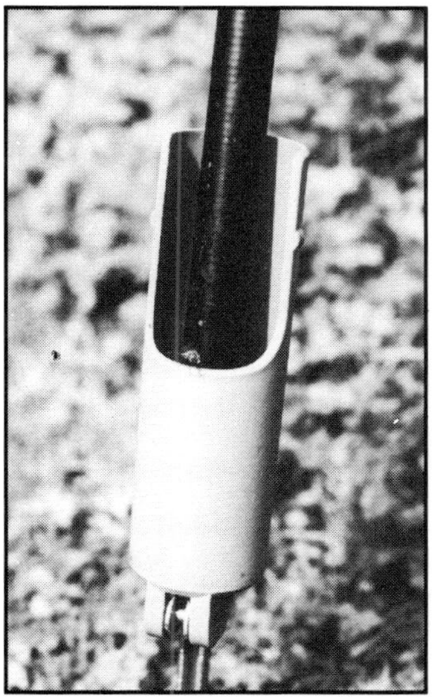

Holder to keep pole and rigs off the ground.

Rest the pole over your knee, cupped in your front hand and pushed down with the back hand. Also keep some pole behind you. Do all these things and the pole can be held firmly and will feel light.

TOP GEAR

Some of the top specialists in the sport were recruited for the Angler's Mail Top Gear series and KEVIN SMITH was a natural choice for barbel tackle.
He devotes most of his season to barbel hunting on the Hampshire Avon and Kennet where he has captured numerous heavyweights into double-figures.
This is how Kevin summarised his approach.

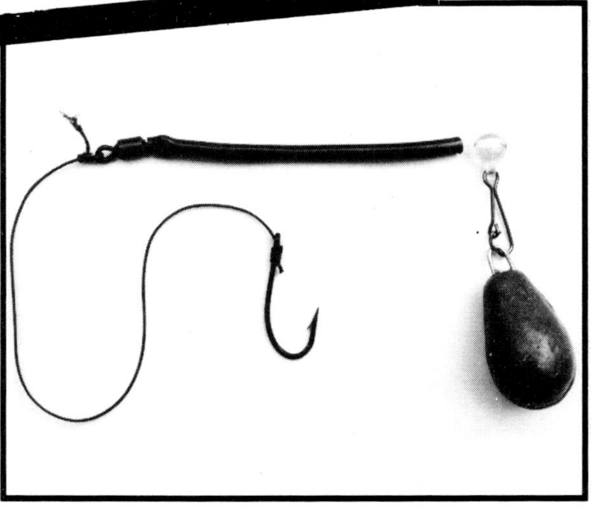

I usually leger for barbel. My hook length is a braided line of 6 lb to 8lb and about 9 in. long. In very weedy swims I reduce this to 3in. to ensure that the hook bait reaches bottom.

I prefer braided hook lengths to nylon because they are very supple allowing the bait to behave more naturally when sucked up and inspected by a barbel.

But braided lines tangle easily with other items of the end rig. To solve this I place a short piece of plastic tubing over the main line between the bomb and swivel-stop.

This separates the hook length from the rest of the tackle during casting and retrieval. The tube is pushed over the eye of the swivel to prevent it sliding up and down the line. Most tackle shops sell similar tubing in their carp fishing department.

I use enough lead to hold bottom–and a little bit more. On some rivers the lead doesn't only have to hold against the current, it must also combat loose weed and debris constantly hitting and catching the line. I carry a range of weights between ½ oz and 2 oz to cover most eventualities.

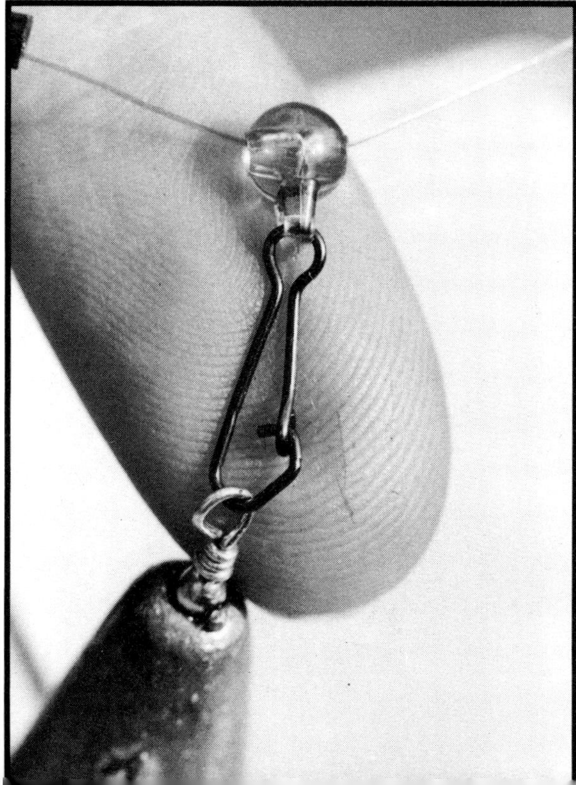

A Drennan leger bead and a link provide a trouble free attachment for the leads. I like the leger bead as the hole has a large surface area around the hole preventing kinks.

I doubt that the barbel ever pulls the line through the bead when it takes the bait. But it is reassuring to know that in the event of a break, the barbel can pull the line clear of the lead and swim off unhindered.

CULT OF THE BARBEL SEE PAGE 93

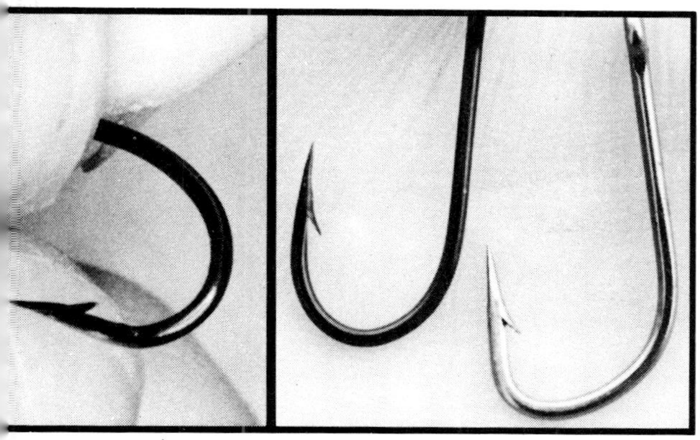

Barbels hooks must be sharp, very strong and totally reliable. I put my faith in Partridges's Jack Hilton carp hooks and Drennan's super specialist in sizes 4 to 8.

I sharpen my hooks before use with a coated metal nail file obtained from Boots the chemist for 70p. It's far superior to anything else I've tried.

To test the point of a hook I run it lightly over the top of my thumb nail. If it's sharp it will score the nail easily.

My carbon barbel rod has a through action and a test curve of about 1¼ lb. It has been adapted to take a slip-on quiver-tip and tip ring. I have fixed beta lights to both the quiver and the tip ring to act as visual indicators at night.

◀ Luncheon meat, corn and tares are my chosen barbel baits. Maggots are very effective on some waters but they are expensive and too popular with unwanted species of fish.

I fry my lucheon meat in a mixture of oil, Bisto and a flavouring such as Turmeric or ground cloves.

Hemp makes a superb attractor. I use it in large quantities–a gallon each session spread over several swims–and fish my hook baits over the top of it.

Tares are simply a substitute for hemp on the hook. I used to spend frustrating minutes' Super Glueing hemp on the hook. These days I throw a handful of tares into the cooking hemp and hook them straight–the barbel don't seem to mind the size difference.

My reel is the dependable Mitchell 300 Pro. It is a sturdy workhorse and should last me many years.

There is no need to carry a lot of line on the spool when fishing rivers. I build my spools up and then add only 50 yards of nylon. Tough rununculus weed and gravel bottoms soon fray and degrade even the toughest of lines so I change mine every other trip.

I carry spools of 6 lb, 8 lb and 11 lb Sylcast. I believe fishing light for barbel is unsporting because the fish is taken to the limits of its endurance before being netted.

TOP GEAR

For on-the-spot baiting I use bait-droppers. They act as a capsule releasing the bait when it hits the bottom. I find swimfeeders to be a liability in fast and weedy rivers.

Before fishing a swim I attach a baitdropper to the end of my line and spend ten minutes or so dropping bait on gravel runs or into holes in the weed. This is followed up with a less accurate baiting with a catapult.

I prefer to fish over a widely spread carpet of hemp and free offerings, casting to various points in the swim.

A large, strong landing net is a must and mine has 36in. arms. To land a barbel in fast water, place the net just downstream of the fish and allow it to drop back into the mesh.

Once the fish has been landed, unhooked and weighed it should be returned immediately to the net and allowed to rest for several minutes in the water. Any photography should take place after this period of rest and with the minimum of fuss.

Return the barbel facing upstream. Hold it beneath the pectorals and by the wrist of its tail. After a minute, remove the hand beneath the pectorals keeping hold of the wrist of the tail. The barbel should hold position in the water. When it kicks strongly let go of the wrist.

Here's a useful little tip. I Araldite a magnet into the lid of all my boxes. I never have to search about for baiting needles. The magnet also keeps a spare hook sharpened and ready for use.

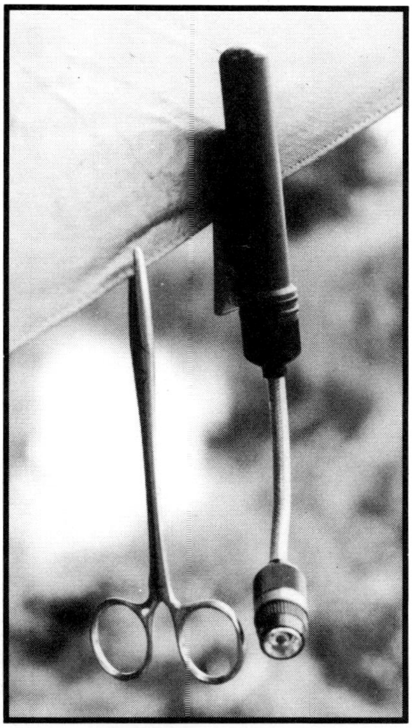

Much of my barbel fishing is done at dusk and into the night. A torch is a must for tying knots and unhooking and weighing fish. Mine has a flexible head and stays clipped, alongside a pair of forceps, to my umbrella or rucksack.

It is important that everything is to hand. There is no excuse for a fish to be left gasping on the bank while you search for unhooking and weighing equipment,

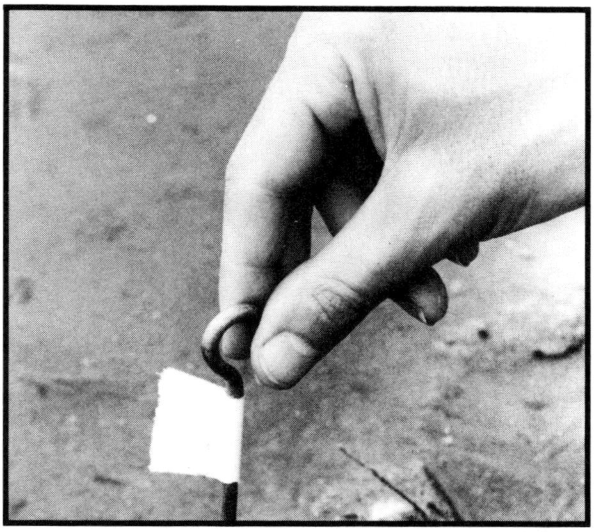

At night I choose a main base swim where I keep my umbrella, cameras and spare clothing. I also like to have several pre-baited swims at my disposal. I mark these with small white flags before dusk so I know precisely where to cast in the night.
The same little flags mark safe netting and fish returning points.

I use rod rests with the reel slightly forward and to the right of my chair. How high the tip is in the air depends on how far across the river I'm fishing. The less line in the water the less drag on the lead.

Barbel are not usually shy biters so there is no need to keep a hand on the rod. But I keep a close eye on the tip. While I may ignore small knocks to the rod top I hit any continuous tremblings as these often signify that a barbel has the bait in its mouth and is holding position.

The landing net is kept ready at a suitable landing point downstream. This allows me to take advantage of the current when playing the barbel and minimises disturbance in the swim.

On clear rivers like the Kennet and Hampshire Avon, Polaroids are invaluable for spotting fish and potential swims.

It is widely thought that brown and yellow lenses beat the normal grey for clarity of vision. But that is not exactly true.

When you place a brown tinted lens over your eyes the sight cells in your brain detecting the unnatural colour shift, work twice as hard to compensate and neutralise the effect.

As a side effect to this process, the extra cell activity also increases the resolving power of your eyes slightly, allowing better separation of hues and detail. The effect only lasts about ten minutes or so, before the brain adapts to the colour shift and the extra cell activity ceases.

To take advantage of this I carry a pair of Optix glasses with grey lenses and swop them with my yellow pair every ten minutes when fish spotting.

I understand that purple lenses are best as the brain never quite gets used to the colour change!

Gary Dunk with an Icelandic Wolf, or catfish.

ALIENS

THE good, the bad and the ugly˜ Iceland's sea fishing has got the lot but is still Mecca as far as I'm concerned.

- **The good...** is the fishing
- **The bad...** is the hard work involved in reeling in hundreds of fish
- **The ugly...** are the specimens which look so bad you nearly jump out of your skin

Two of the ugliest fish locally are the scorpions - known to us as 'Uglies' - and the Sea Wolf/Catfish which were nick-named 'Aliens' by the party who visited Iceland with me.

We flew to Iceland from Heathrow and stayed in Keflavik in the south west of the country, around 30 miles south of the capital Reykjavik.

The bed of the local harbour appeared to have wall-to-wall fish. Dab were the most abundant species with specimens from just a few ounces to 1lb 14oz coming in three at a time every 60 seconds if you could stand the pace.

Rock and pier marks around Keflavik all dropped off to deep water - around 60ft in places - in a short cast of around 20 yards. Large slivers of herring were definitely the bait for cod, coalfish and Redfish (Norway haddock). We also had a small halibut which fell to fellow England international Clive Richards.

The fishing was so fast and furious that it was possible to take 150 fish in just three hours. That won't suit every taste and, I have to admit, it became a bit of a bore and darn hard graft after several sessions.

There is a great deal of potential although a lot more spadework is going to be needed to find the marks that hold the large cod and jumbo halibut.

Boat fishing was something else. Normally a landlubber I eventually had to break out the boat gear after watching parties of six anglers return regularly with 1,000 lb plus catches of cod in three to four hour spells.

It is a decision I shall never regret. It

worked out at around £20 a day each for the charter, not cheap but well worth it.

Gary Dunk hit a large Wolf on the first drift. After spotting its grotesque shape and huge yellow teeth he wanted to cut the line. The skipper would have none of it because this is the most sought after delicacy in this part of the world.

Cod from 10 to 20lb were next to show plus haddock to 9lb, nice pollack and coalfish plus halibut of 8lb. Dave Andrews then landed a 34lb cod, the best of the week-long trip,

The Icelandic scenery is great, the people courteous and friendly and the fishing superb. The cost of living is high and it pays to check out different places before settling on where to have your tea and cakes.

More details of trips from Peter Johannsson, Viking Travel, Hafnargarta 27, Keflavik, Iceland.

Chris Clark catches three at a time and there are plenty more dabs where these came from if you can stand the pace.

AND UGLIES!

...but Iceland's sea sport is red hot, says Chris Clark

One of the many scorpions caught during Chris Clark's trip to Iceland.

TWO WAYS TO WIN A TITLE

IF you're lucky enough to land a record coarse fish then you can seek recognition from two different panels of judges!

First there's there's the long-standing British Record Fish Committee with its HQ in Peterborough. Then there's the National Coarse Fish Record List compiled by the National Association of Specialist Anglers.

You can of course go for both, but the rules are slightly different so read them carefully.

HOW TO CLAIM WITH NASA

1. Photographs of the fish must be available. They should be of good quality, preferably in colour and should be of the angler holding the fish and the fish lying on the ground next to an identifiable object.

2. The weighing scales and/or a Weights and Measures Department certificate must be presented for inspection.

NASA representatives are available to verify a claim.

Stoke-on-Trent angler Tony Bromley with his 1986 record-breaking bream of 16lb 6oz caught from a Cheshire mere.

...AND THE BRFC RULES

IF you have caught a sea fish or wish to enter your coarse catch with the British Record Fish Committee here's how to do it:

1. The body of the fish does not now have to be available but the Committee stresses that because it does not intend to reduce the high standard of proof required, claimants should retain the fish until advised by the Committee.

2. Telephone the BRFC for advice on preservation, identification and claims procedure.

3. Send in a written claim as soon as possible giving the species and weight of the fish, the date and place of capture, tackle used and whether boat or shore caught if it is a sea fish.

4. Provide at least two witnesses or be prepared to swear an affidavit, and get a Weights and Measures Certificate for the scales used.

REMEMBER — ***Angler's Mail will want to know about your catch straight away so give the News Desk a ring (reverse charges) at any time. We will want photographs if possible and all the details.***

NATIONAL COARSE FISH RECORD LIST

	Weight lb oz dr	kilograms	Captor and Venue	Date
Barbel	14 6 0:		A.D. Tyron, Royalty Fishery, Hants Avon	1934
Bleak	0 4 4:		B. Derrington, R. Monnow, Wye mouth	1982
Bream, common	16 6 0:		A. Bromley, private Staffordshire mere.	1986
Bream, silver			Vacant, (minimum claim 1lb)	
Carp	51 8 0		C. Yates, Redmire Pool	1980
Carp, crucian	5 10 8:		G. Halls, Kings Lyn lake, Norfolk	1976
Carp, grass	16 0 0:		K. Crow, Canterbury lake, Kent	1986
Catfish (Wels)	43 8 0:		R.J. Bray, Wilstone Resevoir, Herts	1970
Chub	8 4 0:		G.F. Smith, Royalty Fishery, Hants Avon	1913
Dace	1 4 4:		J.L. Gasson, Little Ouse, Thetford, Norfolk	1960
Eel	11 2 0:		S. Terry, Kingfisher Lake, Hants.	1978
Gudgeon	0 4 4:		M.J. Brown, Fish Pond, Ebbw Vale, Gwent	1977
Orfe, golden	5 6 0:		M. Foot, Kingsley, Hants	1978
Perch	5 9 0:		J. Shayler, private water, Kent	1985
Pike	44 12 0:		M. Linton, Ardleigh.	1987
Roach	4 1 0:		R.G. Jones, gravel pit, Notts.	1975
Rudd	4 8 0:		Rev E.C. Alston, Thetford, Norfolk	1933
Ruffe	0 5 4:		R.J. Jenkins, West View, Farm, Cumbria	1980
Tench	12 811:		A. Wilson, Wilstone Res, Tring, Herts	1985
Walleye	11 12 0:		F.A. Adams, The Delph, Welney, Norfolk	1934
Zander	17 12 0:		D. Litton, Gt Ouse Relief Channel, Norfolk	1977

British Record Fish

FRESHWATER FISH

Recognised as at January 1987.

	Weight lb oz dr	kilograms	Captor and Venue	Date
Barbel	13 12 0:	6 237	J. Day, Hampshire, Avon	1962
Bleak	4 4:	0 120	B.Derrington, River Monnow, Mon	1982
Bream (Common, Bronze)	16 6 0:	7 427	A. Bromley, private fishery, Staffs.	1986
Bullhead (Millers Thumb)	0 1 0:	0 028	R. Johnson, Bramley/Shamley Green River, Surrey	1983
Carp	44 0 0:	19 957	R. Walker, Redmire Pool	1952
Carp, Crucian	5 10 8:	2 565	G. Halls, Lakes, Kings Lynn, Norfolk	1976
Carp, Grass	16 0 0:	7 257	K. Crow, private lake, Canterbury.	1986
Catfish (Wels)	43 8 0:	19 730	R.J. Bray, Wilstone Resevoir, Tring, Herts	1970
Char, Arctic	3 5 0:	1 502	A. Robertson, Loch Earn, Perthshire	1985
Chub	7 6 0:	3 345	W.L. Warren, Hampshire Avon	1957
Dace	1 4 4:	0 574	J.L. Gasson, Little Ouse, Thetford, Norfolk	1960
Eel	11 2 0:	5 046	S. Terry, Kingfisher Lake, Nr Ringwood, Hants	1978
Grayling	3 10 0:	1 644	I. White, River Allen, Dorset	1983
Gudgeon	0 4 4:	0 120	M.J. Bowen, Ebbw Vale, Gwent	1977
Minnow	0 0 13	0 023	R. Merrifield, River Calder, Lancs.	1981
Orfe, Golden	4 12 0:	2 154	J. Moran, Burton Towers, N. Wales.	1986
Perch	5 9 0:	2 523	J.Shayler, private Kent lake	1985
Pike	42 0 0	19 050	D.N. Amies, Thurne System, Norfolk	1985
Pike-perch (Walleye)	11 12 0:	5 329	F. Adams, Delph, Welney, Cambs.	1934
Pike-perch (Zander)	17 4 0:	7 824	D. Litton, Great Ouse Relief Channel	1977
Pollan	— — —:	— —	Open	
Pumpkinseed	0 2 10:	0 074	A. Baverstock, GLC Highgate Pond, London	1977
Roach	4 1 0:	1 842	R.G. Jones, Notts, gravel pit	1975
Rudd	4 10 0:	2 097	D. Webb, Pitsford Reservoir.	1986
Ruffe	0 5 4:	0 148	R.J. Jenkins, West View Farm, Cumbria	1980
Salmon	64 0 0:	29 029	Miss G.W. Ballantine River Tay, Scotland	1922
Schelly (Skelly)	2 1 9:	950	S.M. Barrie, Haweswater, Cumbria	1986
Tench	12 8 11:	5 689	A. Wilson, Wilstone Resevoir, Tring	1985
Trout, American Brook (Brook Char)	5 13 8:	2 650	A. Pearson, Avington Fishery, Hants	1981
Trout, Brown	19 9 4:	8 880	J.A.F. Jackson, Loch Quoich, Inverness-shire	1978
Trout, Rainbow	21 4 0:	9 645	D. Graham, Loch Ave, Scotland	1986
Trout, Sea	20 0 0:	9 071	G. Leavey, River Tweed, Peebles, Scotland	1983
Vendace	— — —	— —	Open	

Species open for freshwater fish claims (Minimum qualifying weight) — **Silver Bream** (1 lb). Qualifying weights are subject to revision by the Committee if necessary.

• *The Editor wishes to thank Mr Peter Tombleson and the British Record (rod caught) Fish Committee for their assistance in compiling these lists.*

SEA FISH (Shore records)

	Weight lb oz dr	kilograms	Captor and Venue	Date
Angler Fish	68 2 0:	30 899	H.G.T. Legerton, Canvey Island, Essex	1967
Bass	18 2 0:	8 220	F.C. Borley, Felixstowe, Suffolk	1943
Blackfish	2 13 0	1 281	A. Dooley, Cullercoats, Northumberland	1986
Bluemouth	1 0 0:	0 454	Qualifying weight	—
Bogue	1 15 4:	0 885	S.G. Torode, Pembroke, Guernsey, C.I.	1978
Bream, Black	4 14 12:	2 232	D.P. Bohan, Alderney, C.I.	1984
Bream, Gilthead	8 2 2:	3 688	A. Marquand, Guernsey, C.I.	1983
Bream, Ray's	7 15 12:	3 621	G. Walker, Crimdon Beach, Hartlepool	1967
Bream, Red	4 7 0:	2 012	A. Salmon, Alderney, CI.	1979
Brill	7 7 8:	3 387	B.M.K. Fletcher, Guernsey, C.I.	1980
Bull Huss	17 15 0:	8 136	M. Roberts, Falmouth, Cornwall	1977
Catfish	12 12 8:	5 797	G.M. Taylor, Stonehaven, Scotland	1978
Coalfish	20 6 0:	9 214	D. Cook, Newquay, Cornwall	1982
Cod	44 8 0:	20 183	B. Jones, Toms Points, Barry, Glam.	1966
Comber	0 12 0:	0 340	Qualifying weight	—
Common Skate	100 0 0:	45 357	Qualifying weight	—
Conger	67 1 0:	30 417	A.W. Lander, Arch Rock End, Torquay	1967
Dab	2 9 8:	1 176	M.L. Watts, Port Talbot, Wales	1936
Dogfish, Black-Mouthed	0 12 0:	0 340	Qualifying weight	—
Dogfish, Lesser Spotted	4 8 0:	2 040	J. Beattie, off Ayr Pier, Scotland	1969
Flounder	5 2 0:	2 324	W. Stevens, Teign Estuary, Devon	1978

Peter Cockwill of Guildford with his Avington lakes rainbow of 20lb 7oz that beat the British record in 1986 — but it was quickly overhauled by a monster from Loch Awe.
Peter's fish fell to a leaded Hare's Ear nymph.

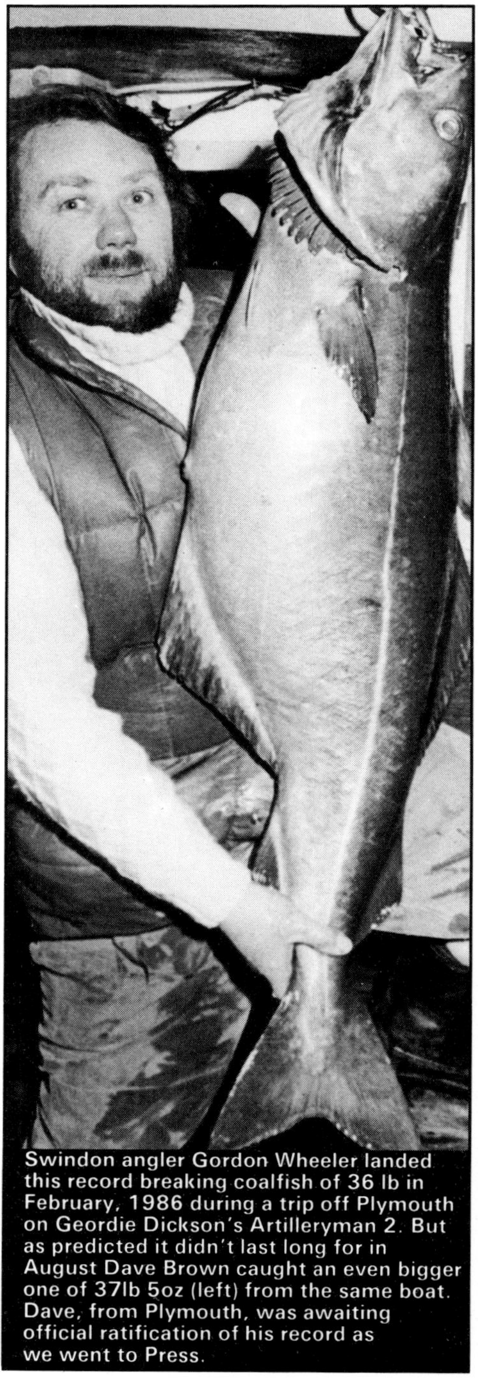

Swindon angler Gordon Wheeler landed this record breaking coalfish of 36 lb in February, 1986 during a trip off Plymouth on Geordie Dickson's Artilleryman 2. But as predicted it didn't last long for in August Dave Brown caught an even bigger one of 37lb 5oz (left) from the same boat. Dave, from Plymouth, was awaiting official ratification of his record as we went to Press.

Sea fish shore records *continued*	Weight lb	oz	dr	kilograms	Captor and Venue	Date
Forkbeard. Greater	1	0	0:	0 454	Qualifying weight	
Garfish	2	15	9:	1 347	M. Wills, Coverack, Cornwall	1979
Greater Weever	1	7	8:	0 666	D.C. Charman, nr. Porthcurno, Cornwall	1983
Gurnard, Grey	1	8	0:	0 680	S. Quine, Isle of Man	1977
Gurnard, Red	2	10	11	1 209	D. Johns, Helford River, Cornwall	1976
Gurnard, Streaked	1	6	8:	0 637	H. Livingstone Smith, Loch Goil, Firth of Clyde	1971
Gurnard, Yellow or Tubfish	12	3	0:	5 528	G.J. Reynolds, Langland Bay, Wales	1976
Haddock	6	12	0:	3 061	G.B. Stevenson, Loch Goil, Firth of Clyde	1976
Haddock, Norway	1	3	0:	0 538	F.P. Fawke, Southend Pier, Essex	1973
Hake	3	8	2:	1 590	W.S. Parry, Morfa Beach, Glamorgan	1984
Halibut	10	0	0:	4 536	Qualifying weight	
Herring	1	0	0:	4 454	Qualifying weight	
John Dory	3	0	0;	1 361	Qualifying weight	
Ling	19	4	0:	8 731	D.J. Rogan, SW coast of Jersey, C.I.	1981
Lumpsucker	14	3	0:	6 435	W.J. Burgess, off Felixstowe Beach, Suffolk	1970
Mackerel	5	11	14:	2 603	M.A. Kemp, Berry Head Quarry, Brixham	1982
Megrim	1	11	11:	0 784	N.A. Morse, Porth Chapel, nr Penzance	1984

Sea fish (Shore records) *continued*	Weight lb	oz	dr	kilograms	Captor and Venue	Date
Monkfish	52	14	0	23 982	G.S. Bishop, Llywngwril Beach, N. Wales	1984
Mullet, Golden Grey	2	11	8	1 233	D. Bohan, Fort Doyle, Alderney, CI	1984
Mullet, Red	3	10	0	1 644	J.E. Martel, Guernsey, C.I.	1967
Mullet, Thick-Lipped Grey	14	2	12	6 427	R. Gifford, Aberthaw, Glam.	1979
Mullet, Thin-Lipped Grey	6	4	0	2 835	H. Mepham, River Rother, Sussex	1981
Opah	20	0	0	9 071	Qualifying weight	—
Pelamid (Bonito)	2	0	0	0 907	Qualifying weight	—
Perch, Dusky	7	0	0	3 175	Qualifying weight	—
Plaice	8	2	12	3 706	N.J. Simon, L'Ancresse, Guernsey	1986
Pollack	18	4	0	8 277	C.R.A. Lowe, Abbotsbury beach, Dorset	1986
Pouting (Bib, Pout)	3	6	0	1 530	W. Reid, Bossington Beach, Somerset	1984
Puffer Fish	6	9	4	2 983	S. Atkinson, Chesil Beach, Dorset	1985
Ray, Blonde	32	8	0	14 740	C. Reeves, SE Alderney.	1986
Ray, Bottle-nosed	15	0	0	6 804	Qualifying weight	—
Ray, Cuckoo	4	10	0	2 097	C.Wills, North Cliffs, Cornwall	1981
Ray, Eagle	15	0	0	6 804	Qualifying weight	—
Ray, Electric	52	11	0	23 897	M.A. Wills, Porthallow, Cornwall	1980
Ray, Marbled Electric	1	0	0	0 454	Qualifying weight	—
Ray, Sandy	2	0	0	0 907	Qualifying weight	—
Ray, Small-eyed	14	2	11	6 426	A. Martinez, Trevose Head, Cornwall	1981
Ray, Spotted	8	5	0	3 770	D.G. Bowen, Gower Peninsula, Wales	1980
Ray, Sting	51	4	0	23 245	A.L. Stevens, Sowley Beach, Hants	1975
Ray, Thornback	21	12	0	9 865	S. Ramsay, The Ross, Kirkcudbright	1985
Ray, Undulate	21	4	0	9 638	K. Skinner, Jersey, C.I.	1983
Rockling, 3-bearded	2	14	13	1 328	F.A. Leason, Bempton Cliffs, Humberside	1984
Rockling, Shore	1	1	4	0 488	A.Bayes, Gristhorpe, Scarborough	1976
Salmon, Coho	1	8	1	0 681	R.J. McCracken, St Sampsons, Guernsey, C.I.	1977
Sea-scorpion (Short-spined)	2	7	8	1 119	B. Logan, Whitley Bay, Tyne & Wear	1982
Scad (Horse Mackerel)	3	0	14	1 384	R. Dillon, Cockenzie, Scotland	1981
Shad, Allis	4	12	7	2 166	P. Gerrard, Chesil Beach, Dorset	1977
Shad, Twaite	2	12	0	1 247	J.W. Martin, Garlieston, Wigtownshire, Scotland	1978
Shark, Blue	40	0	0	18 143	Qualifying weight	—
Shark, Mako	40	0	0	18 143	Qualifying weight	—
Shark, Porbeagle	40	0	0	18 143	Qualifying weight	—
Shark, Thresher	40	0	0	18 143	Qualifying weight	—
Shark, six-gilled	5	2	0	2 268	Qualifying weight	—
Smoothhound, Starry	23	2	0	10 488	D. Carpenter, Beach, Bradwell-on-Sea, Essex	1972
Smoothhound	15	12	12	7 165	G.E. Jones, Boverston, Glam	1981
Sole	6	1	14	2 773	J. Bartram, Alderney, C.I.	1984
Sole, Lemon	2	7	11	1 124	W.N. Callister, Douglas, I.O.M.	1980
Spanish Mackere	0	12	0	0 340	Qualifying weight	—
Spurdog	16	12	8	7 611	R. Legg, Chesil Beach, Dorset	1964
Sunfish	49	4	0	22 338	M. Merry, North Cliffs, Cornwall	1976
Tadpole Fish	1	3	12	0 559	D. Higgins, Whitley Bay, Tyne & Wear	1977
Tope	58	2	0	26 363	R.J. White, Baggy Point, North Devon	1982
Torsk	3	0	0	1 361	Qualifying weight	—
Trigger Fish	4	6	0	1 984	M.J. Blew, Bossington Beach, Somerset	1975
Tunny	40	0	0	18 143	Qualifying weight	—
Tunny, Big-eyed	66	12	0	30 276	Andrew Pascoe, Newlyn Harbour	1985
Turbot	28	8	0	12 926	J.D. Dorling, Dunwich Beach, Suffolk	1973
Whiting	4	0	7	1 826	T. Dell, Chesil Beach, Dorset	1984
Whiting, Blue (Poutassou)	0	12	0	0 340	Qualifying weight	—
Witch	1	2	13	0 533	T.J. Barathy, Colwyn Bay, N. Wales	1967
Wrasse, Ballan	8	6	6	3 808	R.W. LePage, Bordeaux Beach, Guernsey, C.I.	1976
Wrasse, Cuckoo	1	12	2	0 796	A.J. Smart, Alderney, C.I.	1984
Wreck Fish	1	0	0	0 454	Qualifying weight	—

SEA FISH (Boat records)

	Weight lb	oz	dr	kilograms	Captor and Venue	Date
Angler Fish	94	12	4	42 985	S.M.A. Neill, Belfast Lough, NI	1985
Bass	18	6	0	8 334	R.G. Slater, off Eddystone Reef, Plymouth	1975
Black-fish	3	10	8	1 658	James Semple, off Head of Ayr, Scotland	1972
Bluemouth	3	2	8	1 431	Anne Lyngholm, Loch Shell, Stornoway	1976
Bogue	1	13	0	0 822	K. McBride, Eddystone Reef	1981
Bream, Black	6	14	4	3 125	J. Garlick (Torquay), wreck off Devon coast	1977
Bream, Gilthead	5	3	4	2 360	P. King, Salcombe, Devon	1983
Bream, Ray's	6	3	13	2 829	J. Holland, Barra Head, Scotland	1978
Bream, Red	9	8	12	4 330	B.H. Reynolds, off Mevagissey, Cornwall	1974
Brill	16	0	0	7 257	A.H. Fisher, Isle of Man	1950
Bull Huss	22	4	0	10 092	M.L. Hall, Minehead, Somerset	1986
Catfish	24	3	0	10 971	N. Trevelyan, Whitby, Yorks	1980
Coalfish	37	5	0	16 923	D. Brown, Eddystone.	1986

Sea fish (Boat records) *continued*	lb	oz	dr	Weight kilograms	Captor and Venue	Date
Cod	53	0	0:	24 039	G. Martin, Start Point, Devon	1972
Comber	1	13	0:	0 822	B. Phillips, Mounts Bay, Cornwall	1977
Common Skate	227	0	0:	102 961	R. Banks, Tobermory, Scotland,	1986
Conger	109	6	0:	49 609	R.W. Potter, S.E. of Eddystone, Plymouth	1976
Dab	2	12	4:	1 254	R. Islip, Gairloch, Wester Ross, Scotland	1975
Dogfish, Black-Mouthed	2	13	8:	1 288	J.H. Anderson, Loch Fyne, Scotland	1977
Dogfish, Lesser Spotted	4	1	13:	1 865	B.J. Solomon, Newquay, Cornwall	1976
Flounder	5	11	8:	2 593	A.G.L. Cobbledick, Fowey, Cornwall	1956
Forkbeard, Greater	4	11	4:	2 133	Miss M. Woodgate, Falmouth Bay, Cornwall	1969
Garfish	3	0	2:	1 363	J. Nardini, Penzance	1981
Greater Weever	2	4	0:	1 020	P. Ainslie, Brighton	1927
Gurnard, Grey	2	7	0:	1 105	D. Swinbanks, Callach Point, Mull, Scotland	1976
Gurnard, Red	5	0	0:	2 268	B.D. Critchley, off Rhyl, Wales	1973
Gurnard, Streaked	0	12	0:	0 340	Qualifying weight	—
Gurnard, Yellow or Tubfish	11	7	4:	5 195	C.W. King, Wallasey, Cheshire	1952
Haddock	13	11	4:	6 215	G. Bones, off Falmouth, Cornwall	1978
Haddock, Norway	1	13	8:	0 836	T. Barrett, off Southend	1975
Hake	25	5	8:	11 494	H.W. Steele, Belfast Lough, Nth. Ireland	1962
Halibut	234	0	0:	106 136	C. Booth, Dunnet Head, Thurso, Scotland	1979
Herring	1	1	0:	0 481	Brett Barden, off Bexhill, Sussex	1973
John Dory	11	14	0:	5 386	J. Johnson, Newhaven, Sussex	1977
Ling	57	8	0:	26 080	I. Duncan, off Stonehaven, Scotland	1982
Lumpsucker	10	12	10:	4 493	J. McCoy, R. Tyne estuary	1986
Mackerel	6	2	7:	2 790	W.J. Chapple, off Penberth Cove, Cornwall	1984
Megrim	3	12	8:	1 715	P. Christie, Loch Gairloch, Scotland	1973
Monkfish	66	0	0:	29 936	C.G. Chalk, Shoreham, Sussex	1965
Mullet, Golden Grey	1	14	4:	0 857	R. Smith, Falmouth, Cornwall	1981
Mullet, Red	3	7	0:	1 559	M. Hamel, Vale Guernsey, C.I.	1981
Mullet, Thick-Lipped Grey	10	1	0:	4 564	P.C. Libby, Portland, Dorset	1952
Mullet, Thin-Lipped Grey	3	7	0:	1 599	D. Davenport, Christchurch Estuary, Hants.	1983
Opah	128	0	0:	58 057	A.R. Blewett, Mounts Bay, Penzance	1973
Pelamid (Bonito)	8	13	4:	4 004	J. Parnell, Torbay, Devon	1969
Perch, Dusky	28	0	0:	12 700	D.Cope, off Durlston Head, Dorset	1973
Plaice	10	3	8:	4 635	H. Gardiner, Longa Sound, Scotland	1974
Pollack	27	6	0	12 416	R.S. Milkins, SE of Salcombe, Devon	1986
Pouting (Bib, Pout)	5	8	0:	2 494	R.S. Armstrong, off Berry Head, Devon	1969
Puffer fish	4	0	0		Qualifying weight	—
Ray, Blonde	37	12	0:	17 122	H.T. Pout, off Start Point, Devon	1973
Ray, Bottle-nosed	76	0	0:	34 471	R. Bulpitt, off Needles, Isle of Wight	1970
Ray, Cuckoo	5	11	0:	2 579	V. Morrison, off Causeway Coast, N.I.	1975
Ray, Eagle	52	8	0:	23 812	R.J. Smith, off Nab Tower, Isle of Wight	1972
Ray, Electric	96	1	0:	43 571	N.J. Cowley, off Dodman Point, Cornwall	1975
Ray, Marbled Electric	2	8	8:	1 148	B.T. Maguire, Jersey, C.I.	1983
Ray, Sandy	2	0	0:	0 907	Qualifying weight	—
Ray, Small-eyed	16	6	8:	7 441	J. Lush, Off Minehead, Somerset	1982
Ray, Spotted	7	12	0:	3 515	J. Cochrane, Causeway Coast, N.I.	1982
Ray, Sting	61	8	0:	27 894	V.W. Roberts, Pwllheli, Gwynedd	1979
Ray, Thornback	38	0	0:	17 236	J. Patterson, Rustington, Sussex	1935
Ray, Undulate	20	12	4:	9 418	F.J. Casado, Corbiere, Jersey, C.I.	1982
Rocking, 3-bearded	3	2	0:	1 417	N. Docksey, Portland Breakwater, Dorset	1976
Rockling, Shore	0	12	0:	0 340	Qualifying weight	—
Salmon, Coho	1	0	0:	0 454	Qualifying weight	—
Sea-scorpion (Short-spined)	2	3	0:	0 992	R. Stephenson, Gt. Cumrae Island, Scotland	1973
Scad (Horse Mackerel)	3	5	3:	1 507	M.A. Atkins, Torbay, Devon	1978
Shad, Allis	2	0	0:	0 907	Qualifying weight	—
Shad, Twaite	(3	2	0:	1 417)	T. Hayward, Deal	1949
	(3	2	0:	1 417)	S. Jenkins, Torbay	1954
Shark, Blue	218	0	0:	98 878	N. Sutcliffe, Looe, Cornwall	1959
Shark, Mako	500	0	0:	226 786	Mrs J. M. Yallop, off Eddystone, Devon	1971
Shark, Porbeagle	465	0	0:	210 504	J. Potier, off Padstow, Cornwall	1976
Shark, Thresher	323	0	0:	146 504	S. Mills, Nab Tower, Portsmouth	1982
Shark, six-gilled	9	8	0:	4 309	F. E. Beeton, Penlee Point, Plymouth	1976
Smoothhound, Starry	28	0	0:	12 700	R. Grady, Maplin Sands, Essex,	1980
Smoothound	28	0	0	12 700	A. T. Chilvers, Heacham, Norfolk	1969
Sole	3	12	4:	1 708	S. Brice, Fishbourn Creek, IoW	1980
Sole, Lemon	2	2	0:	0 963	J. Gordon, Loch Goil Head, Scotland	1976
Spanish Mackerel	1	0	6:	0 464	P. Jones, Off Guernsey, C.I.	1972
Spurdog	21	3	7:	9 622	P. Barrett, Porthleven, Cornwall	1977
Sunfish	0	15	2:	0 428	T. F. Sisson, Saundersfoot, Pembs., Wales	1976
Tadpole Fish	0	15	2:	0 428	N. G. Davies, Milford Haven, Dyfed	1976
Tope	74	11	0:	33 876	A. B. Harries, Caldy Island, Dyfed	1964
Torsk	15	7	2:	7 005	D. J. MacKay, Pentalnd Firth, Scotland	1982
Trigger Fish	4	9	5:	2 077	E. Montacute, Weymouth Bay	1975
Tunny	851	0	0:	385 989	L. Mitchell Henry, Whitby, Yorks	1933
Turbot	33	12	0:	15 308	R. Simcox, Kingsbridge, Devon	1980
Whiting	6	12	0:	3 061	N.R. Croft, Falmouth, Cornwall	1981
Whiting, Blue (Poutassou)	1	12	0:	0 793	J.H. Anderson, Loch Fyne, Scotland	1977
Witch	0	12	0:	0 340	Qualifying weight	—
Wrasse, Ballan	9	6	0:	4 252	M. Goodacre, Eddystone Gully	1981
Wrasse, Cuckoo	2	0	8:	0 921	A.M. Foley, off Plymouth	1973
Wreck Fish	10	10	0	4 819	B. McNamara, off Eddystone Reef	1980

THE BEST OF BAILEY

You can almost smell the riverbank in JOHN BAILEY'S weekly Mail column. His descriptive powers have earned him a huge following in coarse fishing and these specially selected extracts make it clear why...

War with a sinister scavenger

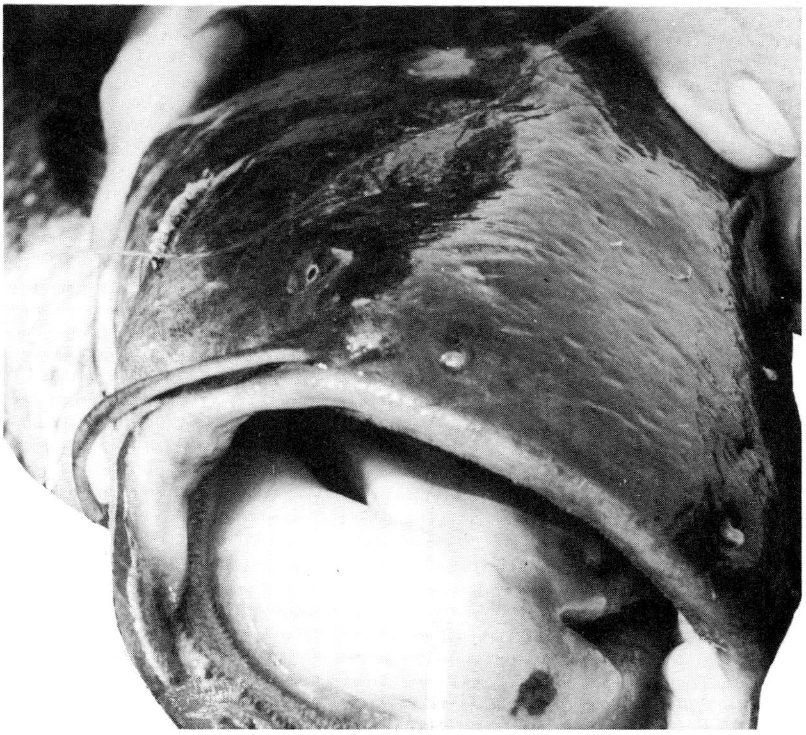

I FOUND the catfish lake with difficulty. It was down a lonely lane, deep in wood and meadow where sheep and horses graze.

My friend, the expert, was waiting by the sluices. Such was the secrecy of our mission that he must remain nameless along with the water - and even the county.

The pool was deathly still under the leaden cloud canopy. The air was warm and clammy. Darkness came early.

My friend had prepared the gear ready for me and I was amazed to find 15 lb line on all rods along with swivels, 15 lb Dacron hook lengths and size 2 forged carp hooks.

Hunks of squid, each as big as a swan mussel were freelined ten yards out, following the lip of the deeps along the dam wall.

Bale arms were left open - for the runs would be flyers. There must be no resistance to these big but sensitive fish.

Evening saw the swallows, twilight the bats and when true night fell the owls took over at last. Carp were active along the margins, big fish some of them, slurping casters and bread drifted in after the roach men had left home.

The temptation to put a bait to them was enormous, but my friend determinedly restrained me. We were after bigger game ....

I had a run at midnight. It was nothing but a pathetically small eel and no clue to the most amazing fishing story of my life ...

It all began on a rod away under the trees. My friend's Optonic sounded. He was at the rod. He felt the line surge along the rings. He struck hard and low and through the blackness I heard the butt creak to the immediate pressure.

'Cat on', he hissed.

'Cat on' — never had I heard those words-or even seen the Danubian wels before. It would be another 40 minutes before I did so even now.

For five minutes, all went well. Twenty yards out the cat held its ground in a sullen stalemate. Though it did not break surface, its deep water struggles raised a continual swell of water to lap on the wall at our feet.

I sensed my friend begin to grow in confidence saying little, but smiling at my questions.

Ten minutes passed and the cat gave nothing to the constant rod pressure that would have crippled most fish-and then it began to move. Irresistibly. Fast.

I had never seen such power. Down an arm of the lake it went. My friend could not follow it for the thickly wooded banks. His line began to catch in the overhanging branches and, at once, there he was up to his waist, wading down the rocking, black lake.

Twenty five minutes had passed. We were 70 yards from the striking place, down in the shallows where the cat pushed and squirmed into the mud.

He bulldozed into fallen branches, threw up the silt and soon the very air stank of heavy, marsh gas.

In the torchlight we saw the line cut its vee from danger point to danger point. Over and over, the fish exploded on the surface on the brink of a snag and of safety.

Thirty-five minutes and at last, at long last, the swivel glided in the torch beam. Something down there was coming in at last.

Now I eased into the lake with net

and torch, feeling the warm water seep over my boots and gradually sinking lower as the centuries of silt gave way beneath me.

A rod length out, a black long body began to break surface. The pressure was crammed on and the water roared.

Still the fish would not surrender. Still it bent the rod to its full test curve and beyond. Soon, though, a whale even would have to give.....

Never will I forget that head emerge. Like a giant bullhead it looked - wide, gaping, and sinister. Its long body thrashed in the net. It was ours. The fight-no, the war was over.

I looked in awe at the near 20 lb. catfish. Nothing in almost 30 years of fishing had prepared me for this: the teeth: the feelers, a foot long, that wrapped around the wrist as I took out the hook: tiny eyes set wide on the flat head: the grey marbled skin of the long body that itself was a cross between a barbel and an eel.

It was truly a fish out of legend, from the dinosaur past.

Cats must be the future of the big fish scene in this country. They are not predators like pike. They are scavengers, the refuse collectors of the fish world and do more harm than good to a fishery.

Water authorities everywhere must open their doors to these whiskered foreigners.

Sometimes it's a right pain!

THE wind drops, the sun sets huge and red in the west, owls call in the woods and the starlings swirl into the night roost.

A carp rolls heavily in the stalking water and a tench bubbles along the margins, moving in towards the spread of corn laid out for it.

After a scorching day, the evening air is warm as milk. In such weather, the only time to be fishing is in the cool and pallid darkness of the short summer night.

Those first three hours until 1am will be the best and will be followed by a lull when the first cracks of dawn bring on new sport once more.

Only when the returning sun has burned off the last dregs of the mist will it be time to leave, perhaps to sleep out the day in a shadowed, heavily curtained room.

Those summer weeks when I live for the night are the best of the whole season for me.

There is a romance and secrecy on the quieter waters. There are good fish to be caught and in this hectic life, it is good sometimes to sit alone with the time and the peace to brood on problems past and present.

At no point during the season are my preparations more elaborate.

I take care to lay out my gear exactly so there is no need to fumble in the dark. I have a hand-torch for hooktying jobs and a virtual searchlight for weighing.

I have clothing for every turn of the weather and rods made up for far out legering and to ambush a margin feeder.

A keepsack is staked out ready and I run through a casting, striking, playing routine while it is still light.

When all this is done, I can settle down, as the light fades, comfortable in body and mind, happy that everything now depends on the fish.

And yet, the night still does show its teeth from time to time...

At Disley Dam, in 1966, at midnight, I poured out a cup of steaming tomato soup from near my flask. For a second I looked in near disbelief through the darkness- the soup was not going into the cup.

I was holding the thing upside down and the boiling liquid welled over the fingers of my left hand. I sat until dawn with them thrust into the cool of the lake water.

The Bridge Lake, mid-1970's-and the choppy water surface and the overcast sky promised good sport. I had extra supplies of groundbait in the dry keepnet behind me.

As was usual there on dark nights, the rats were very active, running over my feet and chattering away in the shadows.

It was not till 1am that I hit into my first fish. It was a good one and as I went to put it in the keepnet, rats sheered away from me.

They had eaten the back-up groundbait-and they had eaten nearly all the keepnet too in order to get at it. A dozen plastic rings lay neatly on the ground and that was pretty well all.

At a carp pit I know, I had physically to place a bait on a tiny platform surrounded by snags and weed, so each new one had to be rowed out and dropped from a boat.

It was 2am, and as I paddled the dinghy out, bait held in my left hand, my wife Sharon held the rod on the bank and fed out the line.

In the darkness she did not see a loop fall behind the spool but she certainly heard me cry out.

In an instant the line had pulled tight and the side-hooked boilie had rammed to the bend of the size 4 hook into the ball of my thumb!

Once, after midnight, I was walking off the Wensum flood plain, feeling pretty jaunty with a couple of 2lb roach under my belt.

There was a cow against the gate to the lane where the van was parked so I gave her a good thwack with the landing net pole. She did not budge. I twisted her tail and she barely moved. I hoiked on her horns and she sat still.

Not till I clipped her on the nose did she give a great roar, rising at once, waving her personal, private parts of a Frisian bull at me under the moonlight.

I did not wait to unlock that gate.

MYSTERY OF THE VANISHING PIKE

I KNOW of a gravel pit which has been stocked with at least two 30lb pike along with another 25 fish between 13 and 28lb.

Yet the pit is a grueller. Blanks are the norm.

The pit is called the 'Murky' because it is constantly stirred by huge bream shoals and a multitude of roach and tench.

So there is a glut of food for the predators-outcasts from a nearby trout lake where they are obviously unwelcome.

Yet, as these big pike go in, they all but disappear. A kick of silt, a boil of water seems, in many cases to be their last goodbye.

What does happen to those exiled pike?

Perhaps they go back in size and condition, suffer trauma in their catching and transportation or fail to adjust to a muddy coarse pit after and upbringing in a clear trout lake.

But good doubles are sometimes caught and they show no sign of hunger or emaciation. They do not look thin, big skeletoned fish that have fallen on hard times. They are doubles anyone would be proud to catch.

It could be that some of these big fish actually die. I do not think many are badly handled, but few people realize how delicate a big pike is.

It might look a crocodile, but its gills are delicate. Its guts are used to being cushioned by the water and on land, its organs are vulnerable.

One accidentally dropped could well die. Only a single small pike has been found dead but others of course could sink to rot unseen in the clouded water.

One friend, a serious and experienced pike man, has suggested that the two pits-no great distance apart-are linked by subterranean channels. He suggests there is a flow of groundwater connecting them that the pike can follow to give re-entry to their native lake.

A more rational explanation is that once caught, the pike here very quickly wise up. For some reason they become unaturally shy and hard to recapture.

There is some proof of this. Often I have noticed bubbles around the float, as though a pike has approached a bait, become alarmed and fled, kicking up the silt as it goes. At other times, there will be a flat around the float as though the water has been displaced by a bolting fish.

Repeatedly, a large flecked tail fin has broken surface alongside the float, and yet the run rarely develops.

The pike that are caught there are barely hooked after halting, short runs. Many come adrift in the fight and not one in my experience has gulped the bait down in a bold fashion.

Another explanation is that the pike here for some reason have developed very restricted feeding times. Perhaps because food fish are plentiful, they do not have to roam long and hard.

Over and over, we have noticed that two or three twenties can be caught in just 30 minutes and that the rest of a week can be quite blank.

The Murky points to the near impossibility of creating a balanced pike fishery.

Where to fish?

THE cloudless sky is slowly turning to gold in the west as I wander across to the tackle shed where a mass of jumbled rods confronts me.

This is it. An evening for fishing and the decision making time has begun.

The options run through my mind. I have an early start at work tomorrow so midnight must be the time to pack. Six hours fishing at most then-so even travelling time has to become a factor.

What are my 'going' waters within 15 minutes? I whirl through the maze of possibilities in my mind.....

Forbidden pool is an obvious temptation. I have weaned good rudd to take well on floating baits.

My only preparation will be some Pedigree Chum Mixer biscuits boiled for 30 seconds or so to the right texture and then flavoured with a dash of maple.

Perhaps it is the flavouring but the fish are crazy for the baits at present.

This is exciting fishing. They take noisily and greedily and although I have not had one yet, I sense there could be a three-pounder in the pool.

If such a fish exists, and if it proves to be as pristine as the others I have caught then it would be the triumph of the season.

But.....the hot weather has been drawing a thick green scum to the surface that has made the fishing difficult and the landing of a big rudd impossible.

If I do hook the big one I hardly want to see it trapped in a clinging blanket of 'lime slime.' No, I will wait a few days there.

It could be a night for Wensum roach. Despite the tragic decline in their numbers, I still have a feeling for a special stretch or two.

The night is warm, the breeze is very slight and the time is just right for a big roach to top and give away its location, indeed its very existence! And, once located these Wensum fish are not so difficult to hook.

The idea appeals. I disentangle a quivertip rod and pick up some breadflake.

And yet.....the summer is the time for action, for bites and for fish. If I do not catch now while times are good then the winter will seem doubly hard. I am not a fanatic. The near impossible can wait for a while!

Our carp water is well on song at present-so tuneful in fact I can almost guarantee myself a couple of doubles or so. Splendid!

After the heat of the day there is a fair chance fish will be going down-I have in mind the margins where the willows and alders give shade.

Still.....the carp lake is just that little bit tame. We know to an ounce how big the fish are and the unexpected is a near impossibility. Carping, tonight is out too.

At last then, there is only one choice left. I take it and pack two tench rods, Optonics and a heavy bag of corn, maggots, brandlings, lobs, boilies and bread.

Tench, after all, are the most whimsical of fish that feed and their preferences change daily-especially on a hard fished pit like the Telegraph.

As I load in the gear I know exactly where I will fish. In this heat, the tench groups bask on a far out plateau, way out of range of the holidaymakers.

When night begins to fall though. then the fish pull into the deep channel that leads around the margins and into a big, heavily fished bay.

I will set down on the mouth of that bay, ready to intercept the tench as they move into graze the six or so hours until dawn.

Ten o'clock it will be when the bubbles first appear to my left as the nightly trek begins. Soon after the tench will porpoise gracefully over my baits and the bobbins will start to stir.

Already I can feel the fight of these big fish in the deep clear water and I known the dilemma' has been solved happily. Or is 'dilemma' the right word here!

Rather it should be 'delight' at the richness of our sport.

Record was hauled in by hand

THE truth behind angling history is often less dramatic than the legend suggests. Sometimes, the catch of a lifetime smacks of a fluke.

The example I have in mind is the capture of a fish that fired me for many seasons-Sid Baker's perch which held the record for years. It weighed 4 lb 12oz, and was caught from Oulton Broad, which at that time was making all kinds of perching history.

To me as a child, teenager and young man, that old BRF record was hallowed and Mr. Baker was one of my earliest heroes.

Admittedly in 1976 that image was dented a little when I happened on his garden pond and saw him fishing and he chased me off down the river.

But then, he had always been known as a character, something of a Norfolk eccentric and this fitted with my image of him and his moment of history.

The story moves on to the early 1980's. Unfortunately, Mr. Baker had died and his lovely home on the outskirts of Norwich was being sold. I knew one of his relatives and before contracts were exchanged I was allowed to fish his garden pond.

It was a lovely place and the March day was mild. Snowdrops were everywhere and the river gurgled past the boundary fence. Some carp began to move, I had a run on the bottom and later, just before dusk, a good fish started to take crust in the remains of a lily bed.

He was not easy, that carp, for after all, a master fisherman had lived just up the lawn and had no doubt given him cause for worry in the past.

It took me a couple of hours and a couple of ruses to hook him, a beautiful mirror, that I guessed at around 8 lb.

I packed up and made my way up the garden in the twilight to leave. There was light on in the house and I called in to express my thanks. Talk about the old record-holder began and the young relation showed me into the great hallway where the great perch hung in a fine case.

First to fish Mr. Bakers pool, second to see his perch, it seemed as though I was living history and had penetrated at last past the bare screed of the angling text books.

Another surprise lay in wait. The young relation knew the story of the capture. Mr Baker had told it many times and laughed loudly at the luck that had followed him.

This, it seems, is how the record perch had fallen.

Mr. Baker and a group of his friends had been doing well at Oulton, capitalising like all good fishermen do, on a bonanza. On the great day they set off, arrived in the early morning and rowed out onto the Broad in two boats.

They all had supplies of small livebaits which they generally fished under a float around the reed-fringed bays of the water.

Of course, the shoals of perch had to be located and jack pike were a problem and I believe that Mr. Baker had upped moorings once or twice before making the golden cast.

Out went his bait and he settled back in his chair to wait. Damn! He noticed an over-run on the reel and a terrible tangle of line in the bottom of the boat.

Gloomily, he set about the bird's nest, never thinking to look what was happening to his float.

It was in fact his boat partner who first saw the bob of red disappear. He told Mr. Baker. No comment!

The line to the rod tip began to tighten but there was still no response from the angler.

The rod actually began to bounce of the gunwhale and still Mr. Baker busied himself with the snarled up reel. Now the rod was being pulled along the side of the boat and crashed into a rowlock.

At last Mr. Baker acted. He picked up the rod and struck. He felt the fish, pronounced it a jack and went back to his knots.

Minutes passed. Still the reel would not clear and Mr. Baker decided the only thing to do was to haul in the jack, break down the whole rig and tackle up afresh.

He stood up in the boat and began to pull the line in by hand, the rod still clattering against the boat boards. Up came the fish-fantastic spined fin first-and the whole scene changed.

No more cursing, just a careful angler guiding a monster to the net and out it came-the new British record.

I do not think I am whispering behind Mr. Baker's memory for he was a great angler and many of his friends and fishing partners remember him with vast affection.

He was a character though and loved that tale as proof that an angler so accomplished could do a wrong and still get away with it.

THE HOTTEST FIS

The striking head of an 8lb Alderney wrasse. Fish well into double-figures have been seen by local divers.

JUST 40 minutes flying time from Southampton Airport is a tiny island paradise surrounded by some of the hottest fishing in Europe.

The place is Alderney - the most northern of the Channel Islands, But strange as it may seem the angling potential is practically untouched.

From any sea angler's point of view, Alderney has something to offer. Its rugged coastline, golden beaches and huge breakwater produce a weekly specimen fish list that no other area of the south coast can hope to equal.

Huge bass, monster wrasse and giant sole and plaice are commonplace. Local anglers regard any sole under 2½lb as something of a midget.

Last season I was fortunate enough to take part in a big wrasse hunt which yielded fish to 8lb 6oz with dozens of 6lb and 7lb wrasse thrown in for good measure.

For those shore anglers wanting something really big then the sand patch behind Fort Doyle is worth a go.

This mark commonly produces tope of over 40lb. To make matters even more interesting far larger tope are known to visit this mark.

Most local tope specialists relate experiences of unstoppable monsters hooked and lost. Some good ray can be taken from the same mark.

One of the fascinating things about shore fishing round Alderney is that it produces good fish right up to late January. The slack fishing times are February to early May and during August. But after August things really begin to hot up. A notable example is the October and November influx of large conger. Unfortunately , on the nights I fished from the Breakwater the big fish avoided me. But individual eels to 62lb have been taken and most regulars have had 40lb fish.

During late November and early December vast shoals of mullet appear off the island. These shoals can often be visually located on either side of the Breakwater and around many rock marks.

Local anglers make a science out of mullet fishing, concocting a revolting soup called shirvy from animal blood, fish oil, bran and chopped meat. This is spooned carefully into the water. Little and

Channel Island angler Danny Le Merrer with a fine 3lb 11oz black bream caught on floatfished worm from Braye Harbour.

HING IN EUROPE

— just 40 minutes from Southampton

Report by TREVOR HOUSBY

Small grey mullet like this are found right around Alderney.

often is the local maxim.

Once the mullet pick up on this groundbait they soon drift in and start taking baits. Top local bait is bacon or raw pork. Individual catches of 30 or 40 mullet are commonly made with fish ranging from 2lb to 6lb.

Larger fish are also present and the best Alderney rod caught mullet weighed in at a magical 11½lb.

Local anglers habitually use very heavy rods for mullet fishing, but most resort to freshwater style tackle.

It is only necessary to work round the island to realise that it is crammed with perfect fishing marks. Most rock marks drop away into deep water while the beaches are also steep too which means that fish can be taken with a short cast.

There are no true charter boats operating at present although fishermen will take visitors out. Most of the best fishing grounds are within a mile or less from the coast. I remember the first time I visited Alderney. I arrived soon after mid-day and by 2pm I was sitting in a boat on a local flatfish mark which I was told was guaranteed to produce fish.

I was sceptical but true to the boatman's word I caught three brill, several blonde ray to 29lb and a 7lb bass.

By 5pm I was back in the harbour well satisfied. Fortunately, I found a local angler who put my brill fillets and bass in a deep freezer. On the day I left I was able to fly these out with me.

Visitors to Alderney should take plenty of spare line and weights. Most of the local rock anglers use old spark plugs in place of lead.

There is a good tackle shop on the island, and restaurants, hotels and guest houses are plentiful. But avoid June to early September which are sell out periods.

Bait can be dug locally or flown in.

Most flights are from Southampton airport. There are also limited flights from Hurn.

Local anglers are extremely helpful and usually do their utmost to ensure a good stay and good fishing to any visiting angler.

• At the time of writing Aurigny Airline run a discount 7 night, 8 day ticket at approx. £50. Some of the local hotels, in particular the Bellvue, offer three and five day breaks which include bed and breakfast and an evening meal. Drink and cigarettes on the island are very cheap as is car hire. Details can be obtained from Aurigny Airlines, Southampton or from the Bellvue hotel Alderney. Make no mistake Alderney is a small island where sport fishing is a way of life.

PARADISE ISLAND — *see colour pictures page 58.*

HOW THE EXP
TACKLE UP

FOUR of our big name columnists collaborated with angling artist Tony Whieldon to produce a series of Tackle Cards that proved immensely popular with Mail readers.

Now we've grouped together all the advice on those cards so you can see at a glance precisely which terminal rigs the experts prefer.

Frank Barlow's

RIVER RIGS

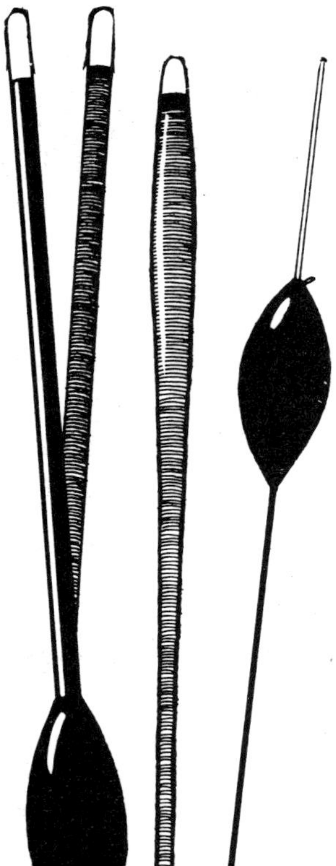

Left to right:
WAGGLERS
STICK FLOAT
POLE FLOAT

The perfect stick float rig for any flowing river. I use a five No. 4 model and string out the shot shirt-button style, breaking down the No. 4s into smaller 6s, 8s and No. 10 tell- tale shot. I fix two No. 8s directly under the float. If I move the stick up the line I leave one No. 8 in position as a guide to the correct depth.

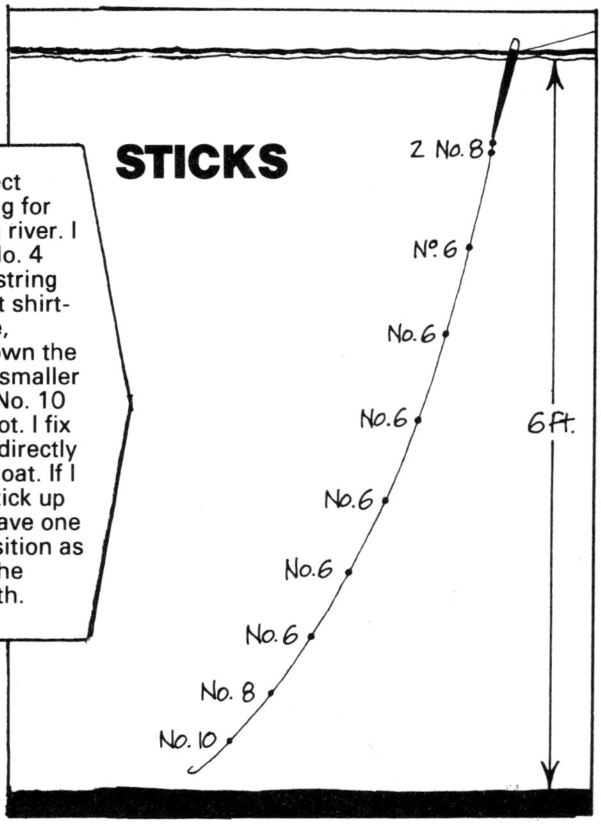

RTS

My waggler rig for swims up to 6ft. deep on the Trent. I use a bodied float for long range when the water is choppy, switching to a straight body if it is calm. I lock, the float with 3 AAAs, two below and one above, to make casting easier.

Notice I leave a ½in. gap between the locking shot. This reduces the chance of bumping fish off on the strike.

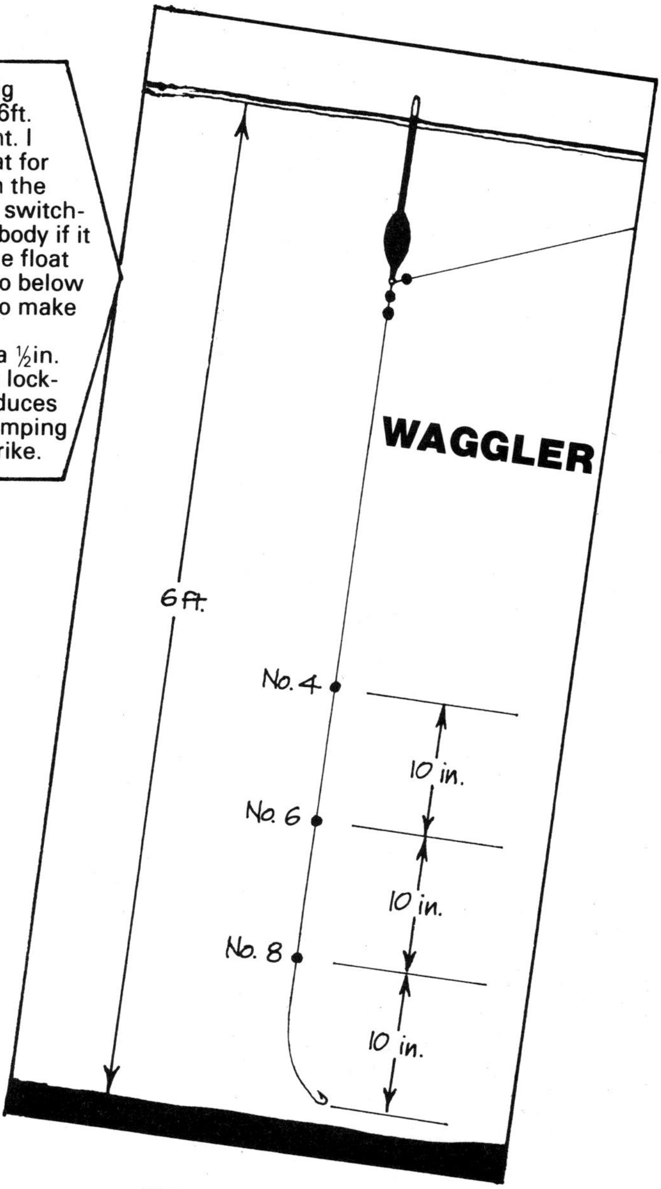

A pole float set-up for when the fish are feeding well.

A 0.75 gramme float is ideal and I place a No. 4 Olivette just below half depth with tiny Styl leads spread evenly below. This allows me to catch either on the drop or hard on the bottom. The tiny No. 12 shot under the float acts as a depth check.

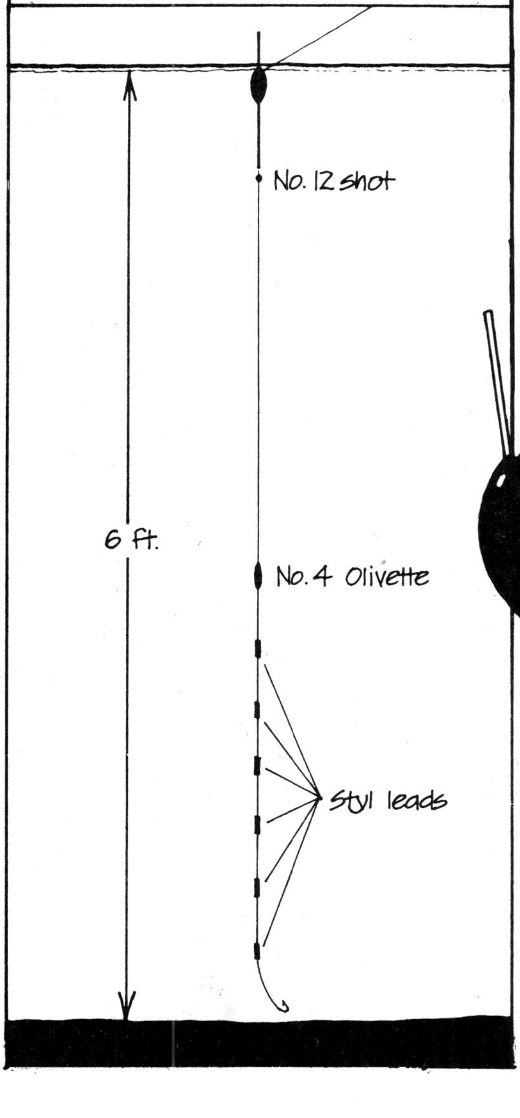

The pole float eye must be in the correct position when fishing flowing waters. When holding back you only want the bristle showing˜ not the body.

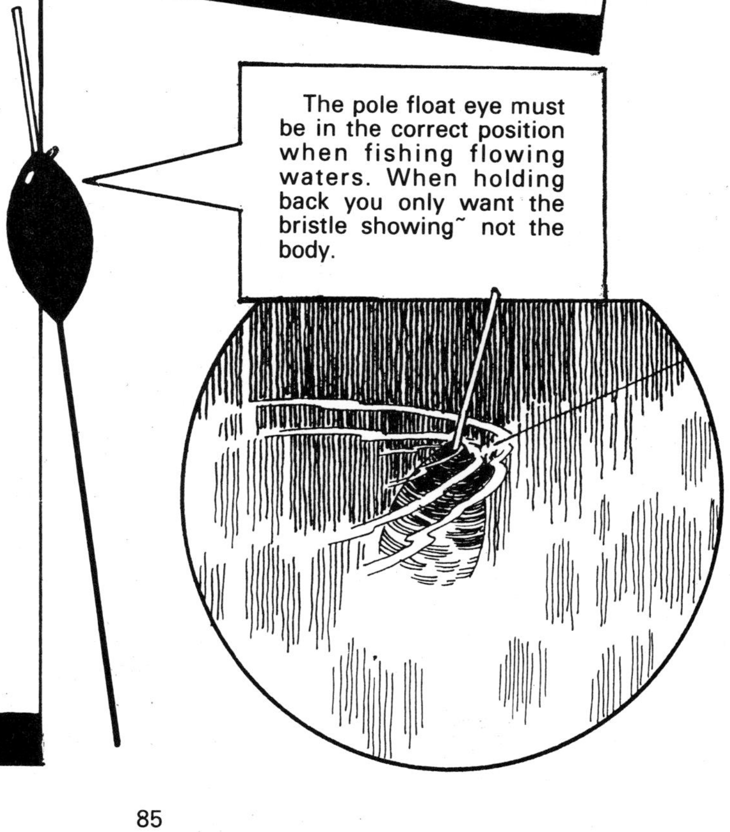

John Baileys BIG FISH APPROACH

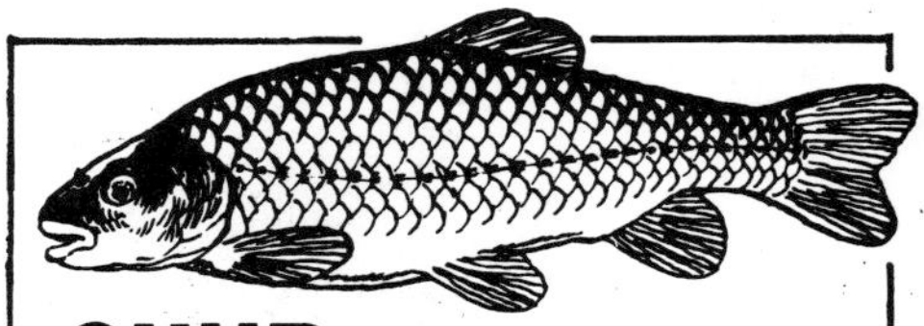

CHUB

In the summer and autumn, chub often prefer to take a bait off the bottom and it is necessary to fish in midwater or even on the top.

I begin by baiting with 2/3 handfuls of mashed bread at the head of the swim. Some of the bread floats but most sinks. After five minutes I follow through with float fished flake.

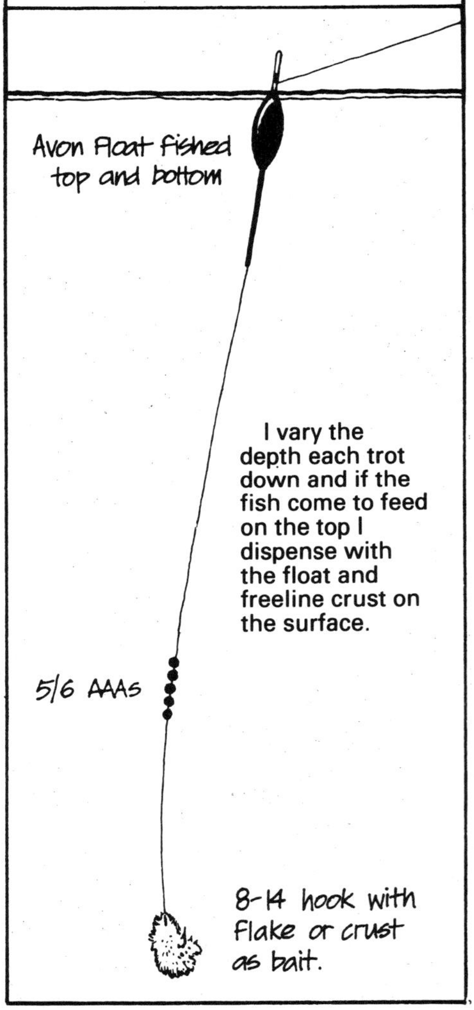

I vary the depth each trot down and if the fish come to feed on the top I dispense with the float and freeline crust on the surface.

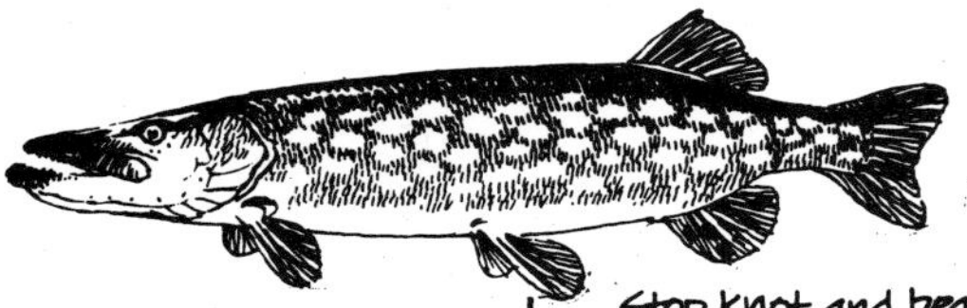

PIKE

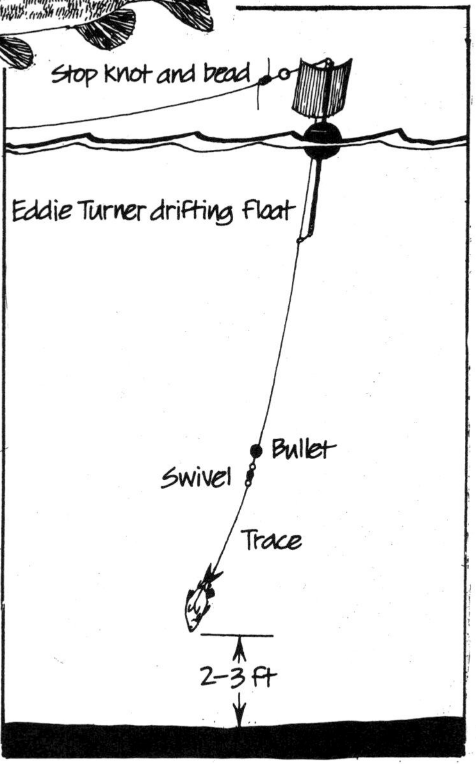

Whenever the wind is moderate or strong, my piking is done on the drift. Trotting a drifting float before the wind I can fish the bait at over 200 yards and reach unexploited holding areas.

ROACH

Weed problems are bad until November, and I have to fish tight into small holes in the weed. I use this rig in combination with a light quiver tip rod and bites often start as a tremor or nod before developing into a six inch pull.

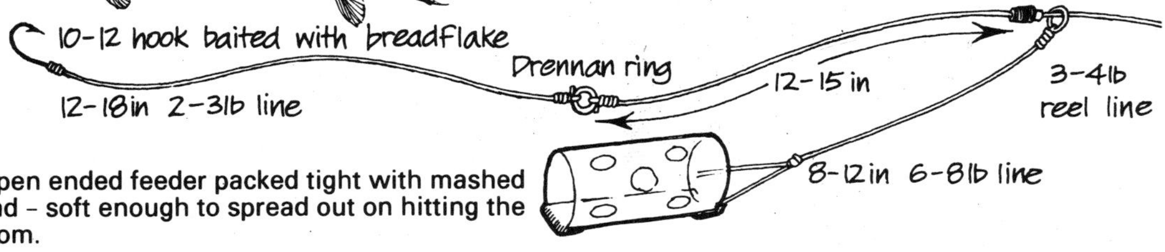

Open ended feeder packed tight with mashed bread – soft enough to spread out on hitting the bottom.

CARP

Much of my carping these days is based around the boilie/hair/bolt/concept. I might start with a standard set-up, as shown below, but I experiment all the time. I might use a fixed lead, or put on a back stop. I might vary the hook length, use a hair or fish a tight or slack line.

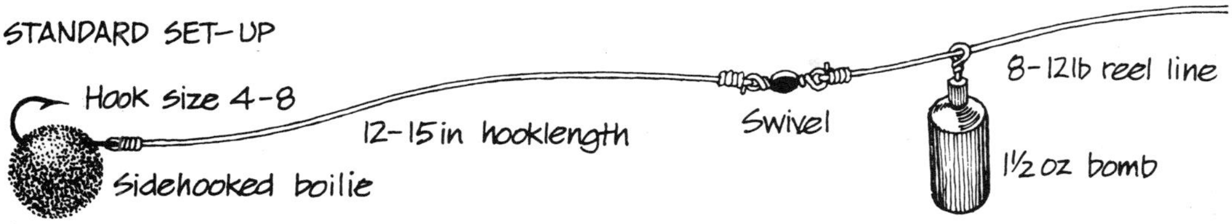

BREAM

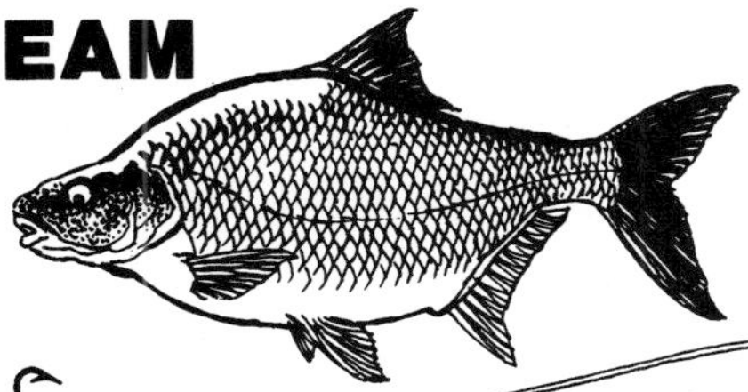

On all my bream lakes, I fish a cross between a matchman and specimen hunter – a matchman at the hook end and a specialist when it comes to indication. This rig produces confident takes to worms, maggots, casters, corn and mini boilies.

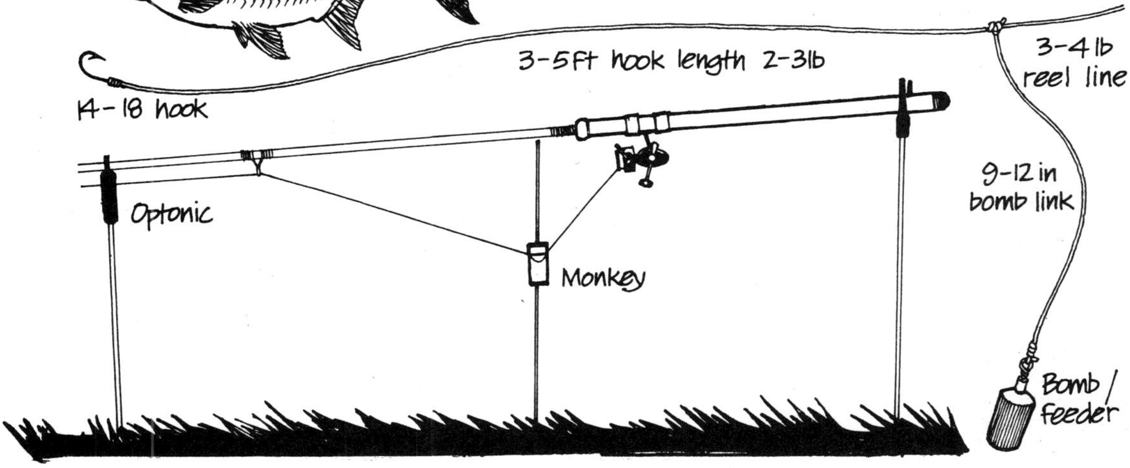

BARBEL

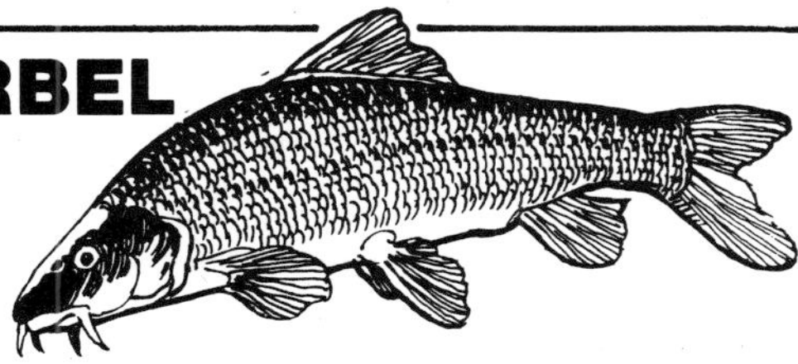

My barbel fishing is done in fast, clear water and it is vital to get the free offerings close to the hook bait. The meat cubes are threaded along the soluble PVA string with a baiting needle. The PVA dissolves and the trap is set.

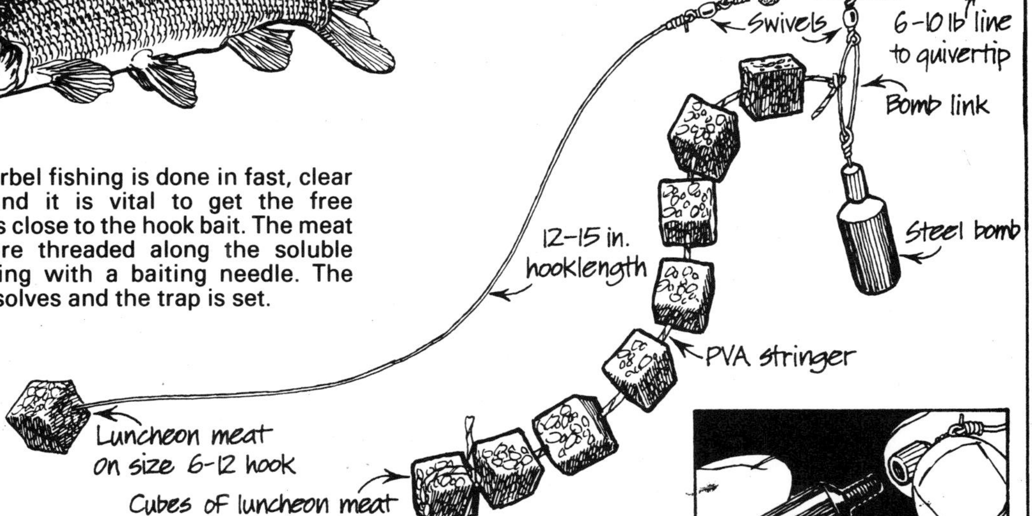

I am very excited about the new steel bombs brought out to replace the lead ones. The new bomb screws into an attachment, so bomb changing is quick and easy.

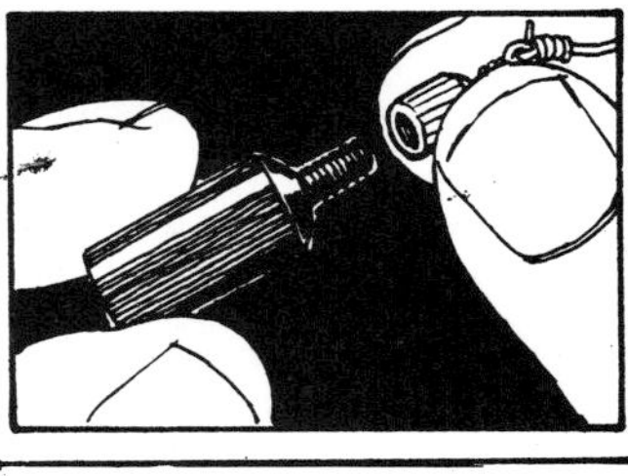

Bob Gledhill's SEA TIPS

FLYING COLLAR SEARCHER

This is a great rig for searching the ground. The bottom end is a conventional hook above and hook below arrangement, with the sinker sliding loose by means of a link swivel. The top boom is a little twisted wire boom with a shortish hook length attached. This is loose on the leader, and on casting, flies up the leader and stops at the knot. This means that two hooks fish together, – the third is up to 10 yards closer in. If you have no leader tie in a stop knot or split shot at the point you want the flying boom to stop.

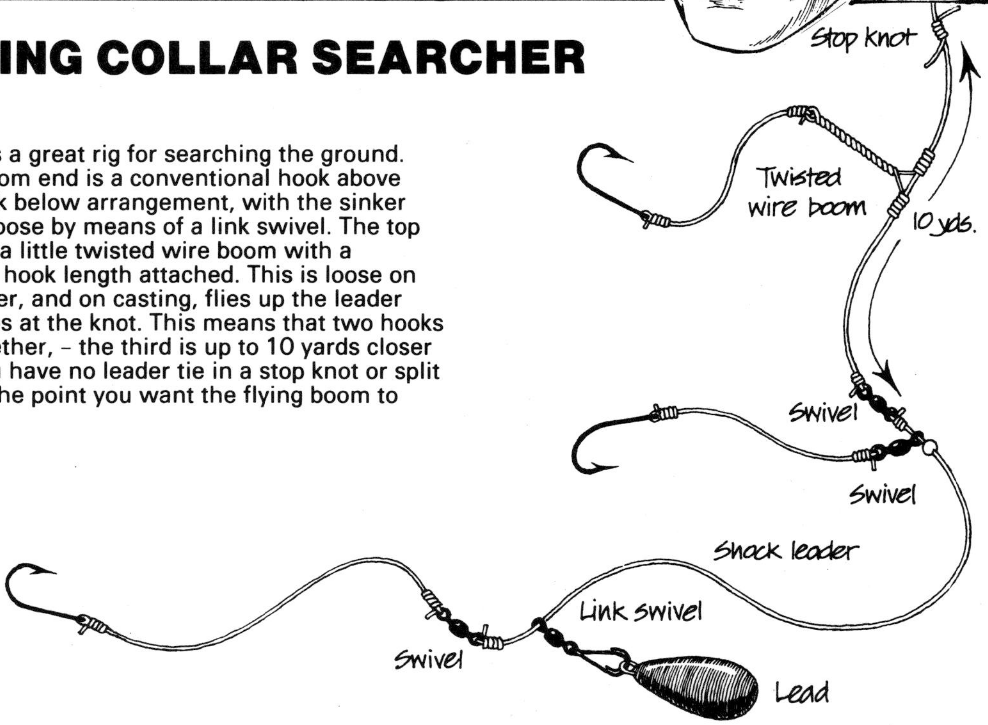

BOLT RIG FOR GALES

This is a useful rig in gale-force conditions for cod, bass or similar fish that will feed in the surf during heavy seas.

A strong grapnel lead is used, and a single hook length tied to the eye of the sinker. This acts like a bolt rig, for when the fish picks up the bait and moves off it meets the solid resistance of the dug-in grapnel, and hooks itself.

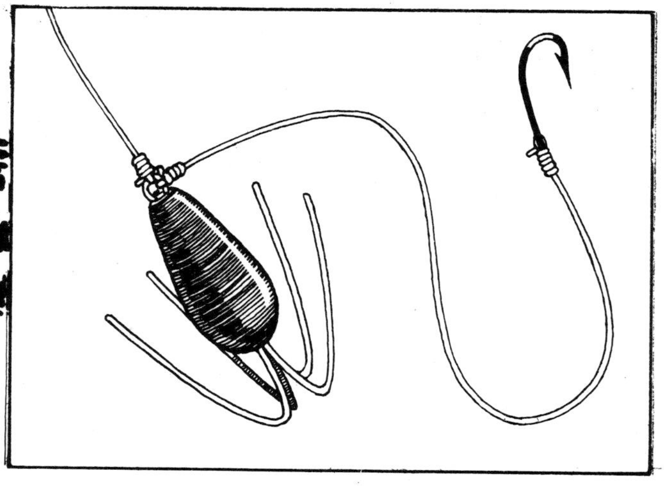

FLOUNDER RIG

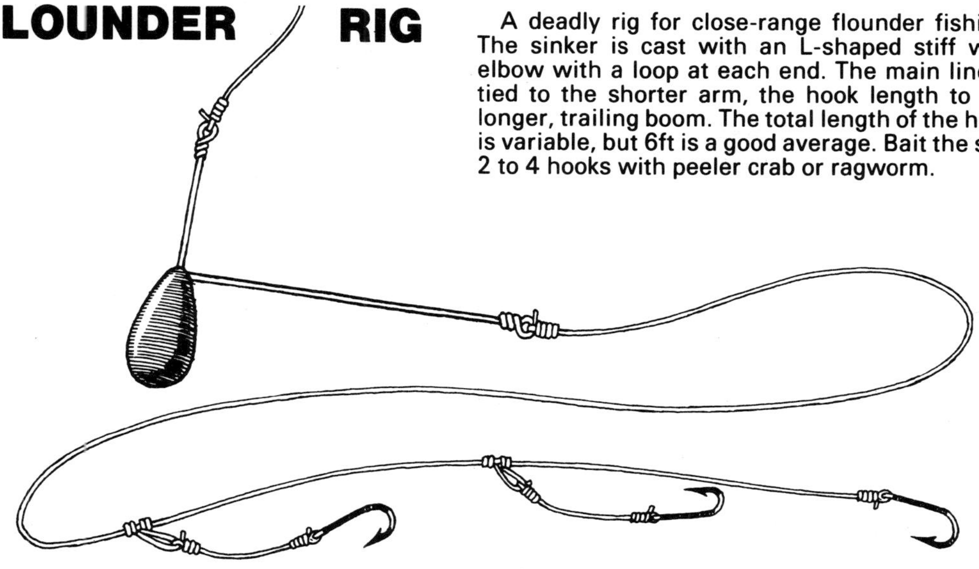

A deadly rig for close-range flounder fishing. The sinker is cast with an L-shaped stiff wire elbow with a loop at each end. The main line is tied to the shorter arm, the hook length to the longer, trailing boom. The total length of the hook is variable, but 6ft is a good average. Bait the size 2 to 4 hooks with peeler crab or ragworm.

ROUGH WATER FLOAT

Useful home-made float for fishing in choppy water or at a distance. Glue a stem of thin dowel into a wire cork and whip an eyelet on the bottom of the stem. Make a flag from sticky vinyl tape folded over.

The float is positioned with a split shot either side. Weight to cock the float is best done using spiral barrel leads or a separate dropper with a little bomb weight attached. Good rig for pollack, coalfish and wrasse.

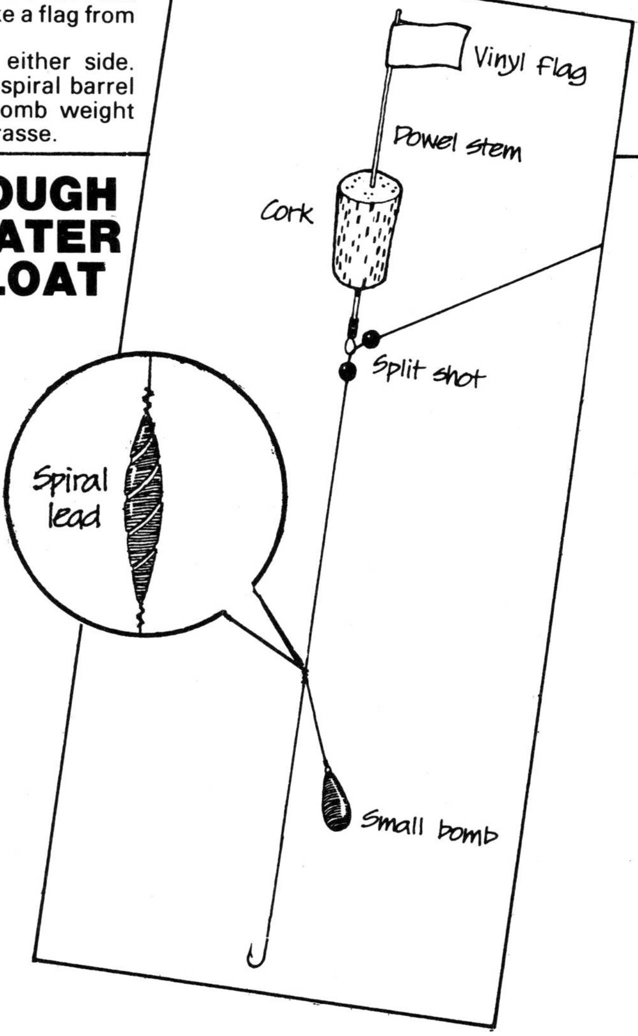

TANGLE BEATER

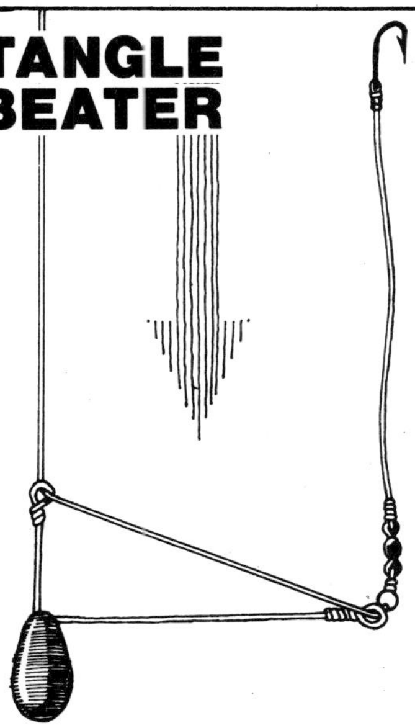

Avoid tangles with this rig when fishing from a boat into deep water. The sinker has a stiff wire elbow in it. When the rig descends the boom holds the hook length away from the main line and sinker, and avoids annoying snarl-ups.

This is an easy sinker to make and it works with any weight or shape you like.

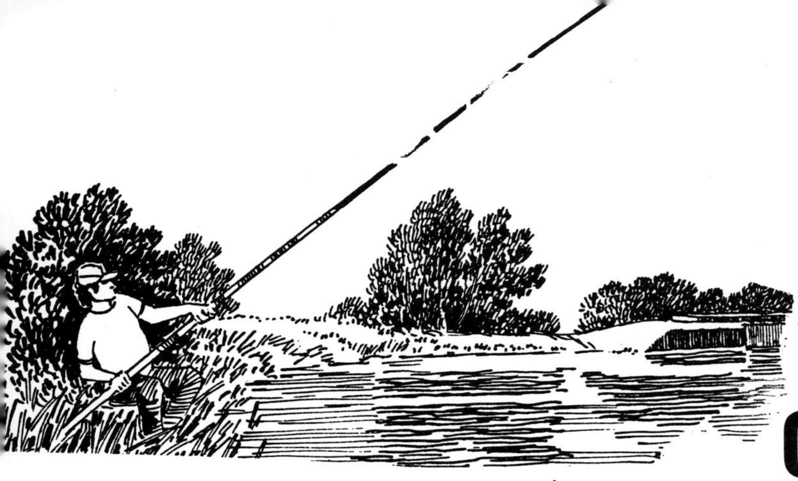

Dave Coster's STILLWATER SET-UPS

SHALLOWS RIG

This is my shallow water, far bank canal rig for caster or maggot fishing. The float is my own design – green dyed sarkandas reed for the body with a fine cane cocktail stick insert for the most delicate bites.

I use green dye to saturate the reed body, dry it off and then apply varnish. This way my floats don't chip should I accidently hit the far side piling.

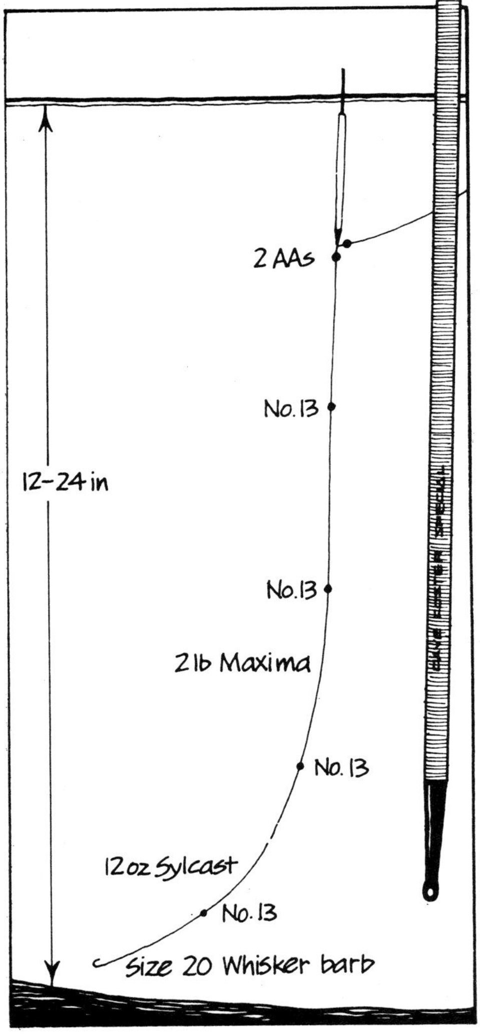

POLE AND BLOODWORM RIG

This is my favourite Grand Union Canal bloodworm and breadpunch rig. The Olivette is always positioned well up around mid-depth. The float has a very nice stabilising wire stem and cocks very quickly, making it superb for speed work. I usually allow three to four feet of line from the float to the pole tip, so the float is presented at least a couple of feet away from the end of the pole. This prevents cagey fish being spooked by movement of the pole.

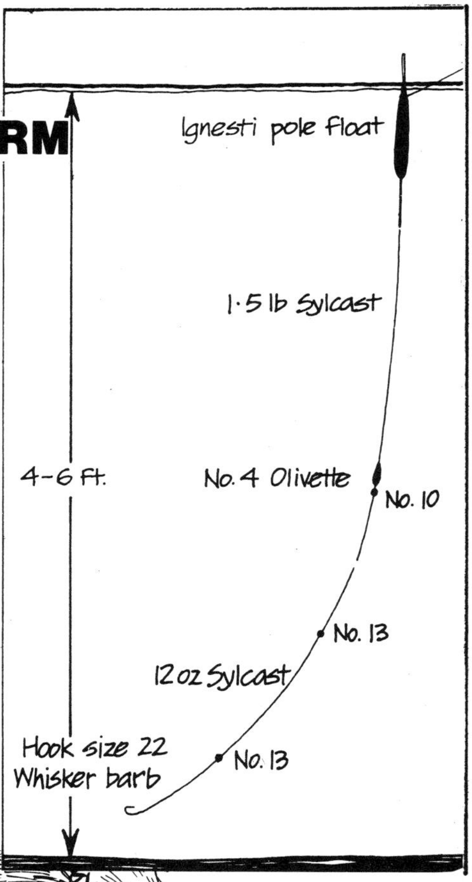

DRIFT-BEATER

Here's a long range stillwater drift beating rig. If the drift is really bad I trim a little bit off the locking shot and put several No. 11s, shirt button style, on the hooklength – these act as a drag and stop the float from trotting through the swim too quickly.

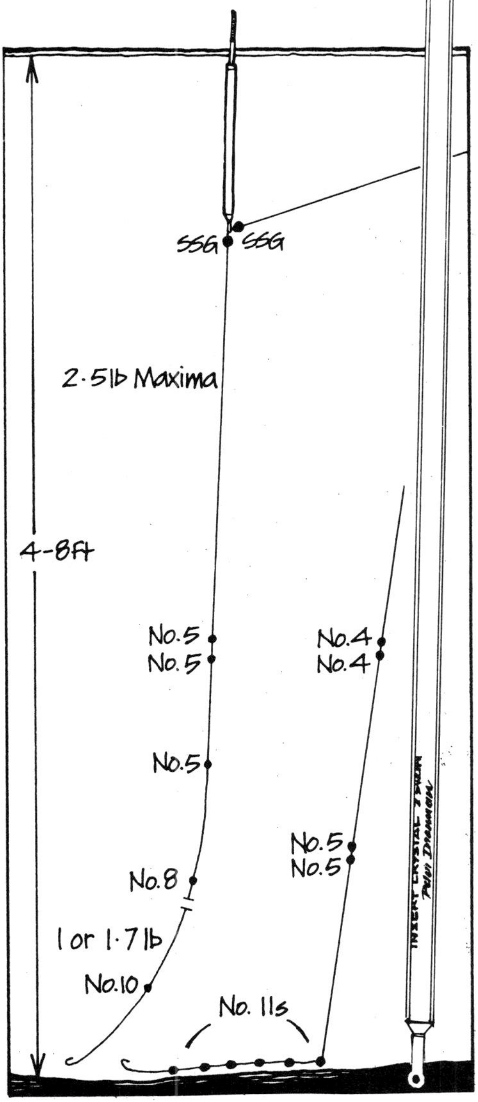

This is my big fish long pole rig. I've landed carp to 6lb 10oz on it and tench to nearly 5lb so I know it works! The No.4 shot are often moved around, especially on weedy waters. I use the eyed hook design as a precaution should a big fish charge into a weed bed – with spade end designs the sharp spade cuts through the line under such impact.

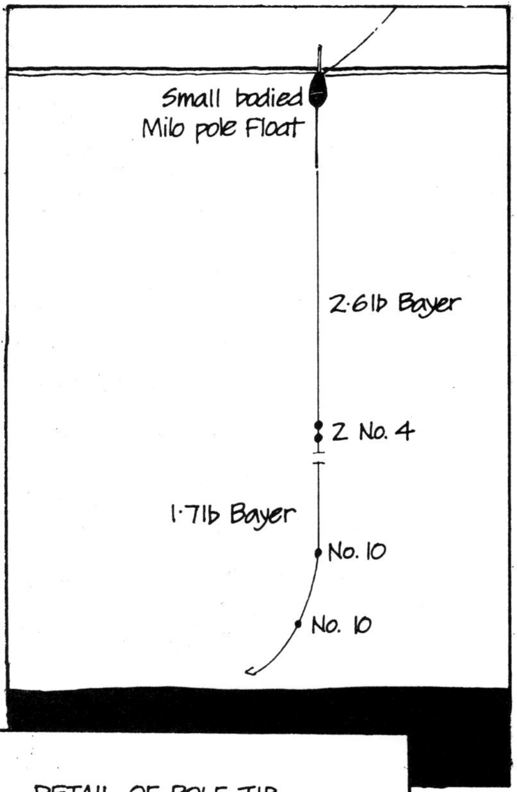

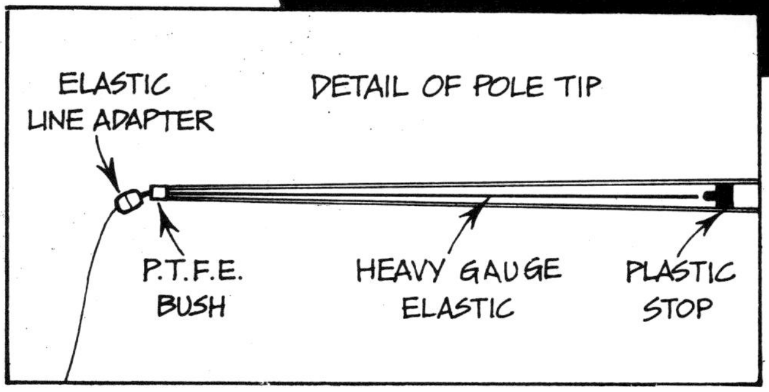

tony Whieldon

TANGLE-FREE BOMB LOOP

I've become something of a quiver tip fanatic over the past year and this bomb rig is a further development from using the loop method when feeder fishing. What I like about it is that there are no top shot or leger stops involved, so I rarely have tangles. A taking fish has up to 18 inches of line to pull through the snap swivel before hitting resistance, but of course I strike long before that happens.

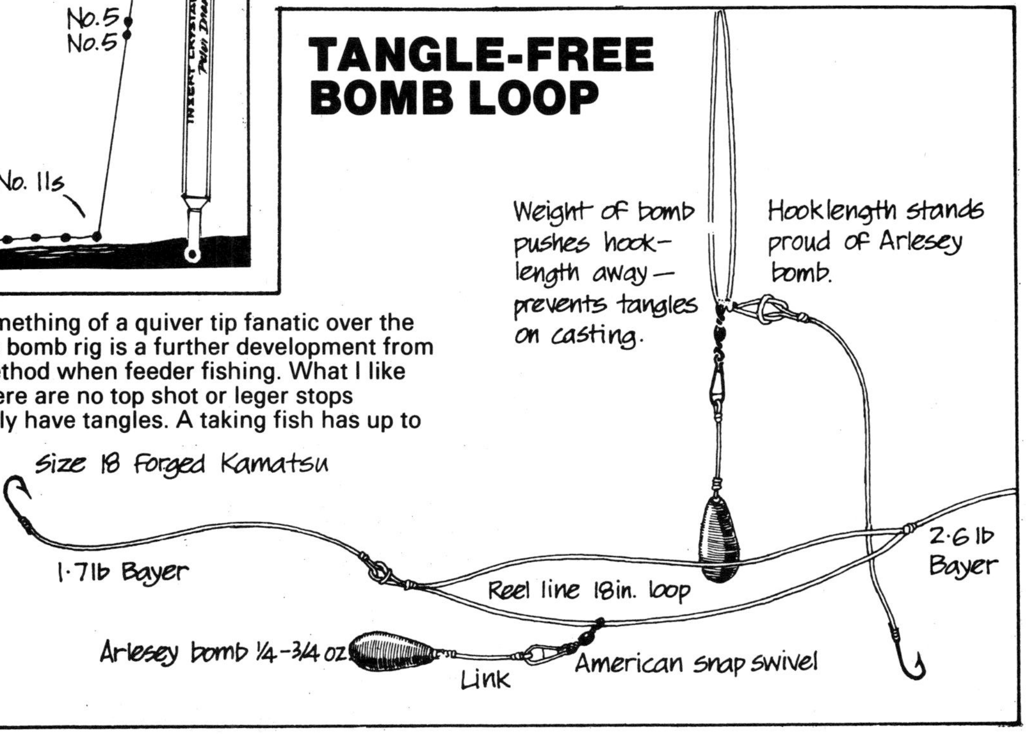

DROUGHT WAS A BLESSING IN DISGUISE

Marsworth towpath where the carp have become a major attraction.

Easy does it. Chris Smith of Bromages match group steers a chunky little common away from the far bank boats.

THE Grand Union Canal at Marsworth in Buckinghamshire used to be a mediocre cut until it was struck by drought ten years ago.

But following the long, hot summer of 1976 the canal was topped up with water from the neighbouring Marsworth Reservoir and thousands of carp found their way into the canal at the same time.

It was not until the start of the 1977 season that Tring Anglers members discovered their windfall. From then on it was fish a chuck and some of the best sport any of the locals had ever experienced.

In 1978 it was Aylesbury matchman Mike Smith who dominated the Marsworth matches and fishing bread with the float he ruled supreme through to 1980.

Next it was London angler Billy Allen and Dennis Dixon from Hertfordshire who made an impact. The pair were frequent winners on other parts of the canal with chub and the same methods brought them money in the Marsworth matches.

The carp packed on weight and fighting power as every season passed and at one time locals were concerned that they had taken over at the expense of other species.

But during the last two or three years things have evened out. The carp are now averaging 2 to 3 lb and happily share overhanging bushes, the hulls of boats and underwater tree roots with roach to 1½lb, perch to 2½lb and 4lb bream.

There are no shortage of matches at Marsworth. Keith Pauling, the Tring Anglers Open match organiser and a local tackle dealer, says: 'I never have any trouble selling tickets for my matches. The place has such a good reputation they always sell out within two days of the event being advertised in Angler's Mail.'

Essex anglers have a very good track record on this venue and it was Angling Centre matchman and Essex County star Richard Bambury who set the match record with a 34lb haul.

Several specimen carp catches have been reported from the stretch but the biggest authenticated fish was a 19-pounder caught in 1984.

Day tickets are available from the bailiff on the bank which for a little bit of carp fishing paradise can't be bad.

DAN PFEIFFER.

West London angler Pete Hawley slips a hard fighting Grand Union mirror in his net.

FRED CROUCH has fished exclusively for barbel since 1956. That's 30 years of devotion to a single species! Here he explains why barbel are so special to him...

CULT OF THE BARBEL

WHEN I caught my first barbel in 1956 most of my angling pals had never seen one, let alone experienced the thrill of hooking this exciting fish.

But since that time these aristocrats of the river have become so widespread that they are now within fairly easy reach of most anglers.

I think the main reason for the barbel's increasing popularity is its sheer power, Few coarse fish are capable of equalling its fighting ability pound for pound, especially in the middle weight range of 4 to 8 lb.

Add to this its somewhat mysterious lifestyle and it is easy to understand why it attracts such a fast growing band of followers.

Nowadays, methods of bait presentation inevitably demand greater imagination for the barbel's ability to 'learn from its mistakes' can frustrate the sloppy approach.

Bottom loving, this scavenger of the river bed can go almost unnoticed - even in clear water - as it furtively glides in and out of cover. Often, when all seems quiet it will take a bait with such sudden ferocity that even the most experienced angler can be taken completely by surprise.

Truly omniverous, barbel use their specialised features to search out their food in weed beds and between stones on the gravelly river beds.

While they can be termed 'group fish', they are not shoal fish as such and only gather in large numbers at spawning time.

It is true that they can be enticed into forming shoals, but that would be because the angler is offering a concentration of food particles, something that very rarely occurs in the barbel's natural world.

They can often be observed foraging around singly in a leisurely fashion as do many species of animals and birds when left undisturbed. But this normal behavioural routine suddenly disappears when a concentration of food is encountered - think of the chaos on a well stocked bird table!

That's when the competitive instinct emerges and seemingly driven by the fear of missing out, large groups of barbel can become almost suicidal as each fish tries to get its share of the bounty, the result of which is normally a good day for the angler.

Unfortunately it is not always

Fred has hooked hundreds of barbel like this from the Hampshire Avon but the thrill never wanes.

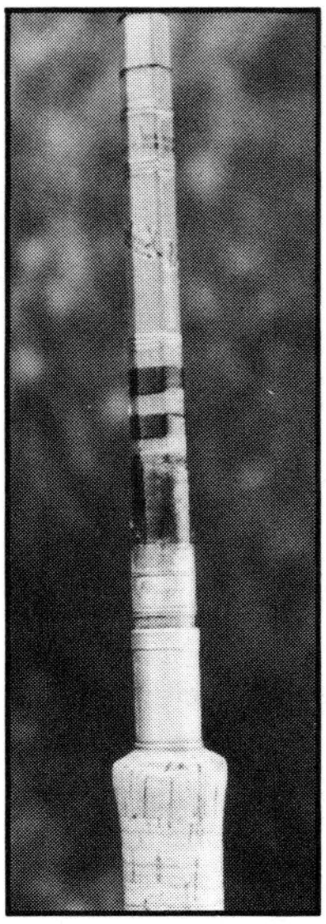

Split-cane rod and Aerial centrepin...you'll never see Fred Crouch with anything else on the riverbank. He reckons modern tackle just doesn't compare.

possible to create this situation. When barbel are feeding as nature intended they're much harder to fool and the angler must be content with a smaller number of fish.

A poorly presented bait will often bring about the downfall of small uneducated fish, but to consistently fool the wiser ones the angler needs to be aware of the barbel's ability to programme itself to constant dangers.

The old myth that barbel go around the river bed behaving like vacuum cleaners has been dispelled forever.

Our whiskered friend takes in its items of food on most occasions with great deliberation.

I get great satisfaction when I examine the mouths of my fish to discover the lips unmarked. This indicates that the fish hasn't been caught recently or regularly.

If notes are kept of these tell-tale marks it can give a very good guide as to whether the methods employed are proving more effective than normal. Simply catching large numbers of barbel doesn't mean that everything is as good as it could be.

There is something extra pleasing about watching a perfectly conditioned fish slide over the rim of the landing net.

Barbel are inherently nomadic fish and for various reasons can leave certain areas and relocate in other stretches. On impounded lengths of the river they will obviously be limited in their choice of abode, but where no such restrictions occur they can travel great distances.

Many times over the years I have been aware of quite heavily populated areas becoming almost devoid of barbel only to return to their former densities a season or two later.

There are, of course, explanations for this, such as changing patterns of weed growth and varying water levels. But the chief factor is food availability and the fish's natural learning ability.

In very popular areas the barbel gradually react to the threat from the angler by becoming more reluctant to feed. As this happens the anglers move on to other swims where they won't have the same frightening effect on the fish which regroup in response to the food and the cycle repeats itself.

Since the late 1950's I have noticed a great change in angler's attitude to the barbel.

From almost total apathy to the present day intense interest, this dogged fighter's rise from the bottom to the top of the popularity chart fills me with delight.

Wherever barbel exist the vast majority of anglers are no longer content to fish for what comes along, but set their stalls out purely with barbel in mind.

One result of this is absolutely certain - the barbel population will continue to increase.

I always get great pleasure in taking people out who have never caught a barbel and watching their expressions change to total disbelief as a fish threatens furiously to demolish their tackle.

I would estimate that 90 per cent of anglers that I have introduced to barbel fishing have been very quickly and solidly converted to the species and whereas they don't necessarily forsake other types of angling, they are never happier than when pitting their wits against this somewhat elusive fish.

On one occasion I took carp angler Gerry Savage of Radio London to the Avon in the hope of fulfilling his lifetime ambition to catch a barbel. All of his previous attempts had ended in failure, but we were fortunate and he landed a fish of 6 lb 2 oz.

The sheer pleasure and excitement that he experienced was heard by his many thousands of listeners. This is just one of the super memories that made my last three decades of barbel fishing such a memorable period.

My decision to devote my entire angling interest to barbel may, appear rather extreme. But I haven't a single regret and if I could turn back the clock 30 years I would make the same choice again.

There has been a marked change during the last 25 years in the tackle employed. The fish's power and snaggy environment used to prompt experts to recommend strong rods, large hooks and very heavy lines.

Modern technology and a much greater understanding of the hooked barbel's behaviour have encouraged finesse and skill to replace brute strength thus increasing excitement and pleasure available through the use of finer tackle.

A 1¼ lb test curve rod and centre pin reel carrying 5 lb line can, in

Plastic baitdropper designed by Fred Crouch. It's vital for depositing loose feed with pinpoint accuracy.

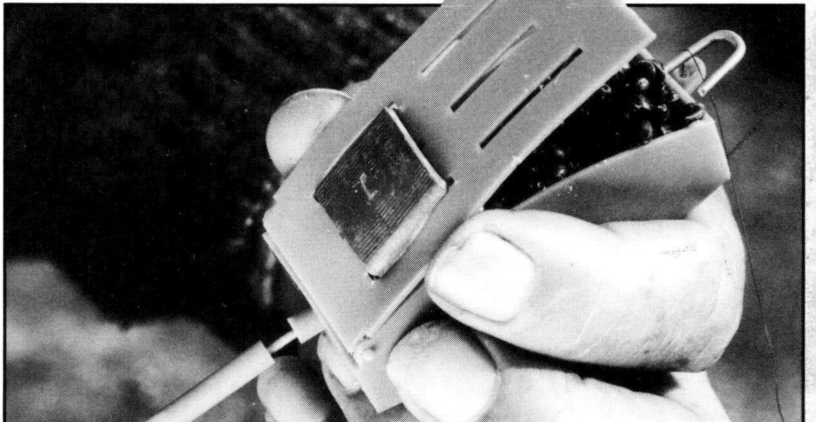